A BIBLICAL PERSPECTIVE OF THE MARTIAL ARTS

ROBERT BUSSEY

CROSSTRAINING
PUBLISHING

A BIBLICAL PERSPECTIVE OF MARTIAL ARTS

Robert Bussey, A Biblical Perspective of Martial Arts

ISBN 1-887002-43-X

Cross Training Publishing
1604 S. Harrison St.
Grand Island, NE 68803
(308) 384-5762

This book is manufactured in the United States of America.

Library of Congress Cataloging in Publication Data in Progress.

Published by Cross Training Publishing,
1604 S. Harrison Street
Grand Island, NE 68803
1-800-430-8588

DEDICATION

To my father, Howard P. Bussey, whom I love and respect with all of my heart. You have shown me the importance of an easy going manner and persevering spirit.

ACKNOWLEDGMENTS

So many folks have influenced my writing this book, and I wish I could name them all. I gratefully acknowledge the thousands of members associated with my teachings around the world for their hunger, desire, and dedication to the truth. To the members of my immediate family, especially Kathy, I thank you. With delight, I recognize Jim Rosenbach and family, as well as all those who have stood by me in times of crisis, serving me with counsel and support. I thank Bob and Cynthia Jensen, Steve and Debbie Bowers, Jeff McKissack, Chris Doner, Bill Dow, Robert Rieth, Gordon Thiessen, and the staff at Cross Training Publishing for their encouragement and hard work. Finally, to the greatest gifts the Lord has privileged me with, Hilary and Collin, my two children, with whom I have not the words to express my love for them.

CONTENTS

INTRODUCTION

When I was 9 years old, I became fascinated with the concept of being able to use my hands and feet as a means of self-defense, after reading a karate magazine from cover to cover. I was small for my age and frightened of the world that surrounded me in the turbulent 1960s. When I was 11, my parents enrolled me in a martial arts class along with my brothers. In less than a month, I was not only hooked, but knew beyond a shadow of a doubt that I wanted to dedicate my life to the study of the ancient arts.

I was instructing at 14, and opened my first of several commercial schools at the age of 15, along with a business partner and best friend. Over the course of years, I gained some notoriety by venturing into numerous styles, and achieving black belt degrees, while literally fighting my way to the top of the game. I lived and breathed the martial arts and vowed to myself to be the best that I could be. There seemed to be no remedy for my obsession for skill and knowledge.

After travelling overseas in search of the ultimate master, I survived dark alley fights in South Korea, and rigorous training and hardships in Japan. On one trip to the Orient, I was hospitalized and almost died. I mastered ancient techniques and became licensed in systems never before taught to non-orientals. In fact, by the age of 24, I was running the largest Ninja training facility in the world. I was chastised by martial arts' masters in my community because of my youth, and at one point, was challenged to a death match by an Okinawan Sensei.

Through all of this, including numerous broken bones and surgeries, this search for knowledge and technique never quenched the hunger I felt for things deeper than tangible battle skills. Beyond basic attainable attributes associated with martial arts like self-discipline, confidence, and fitness, I wanted more. Years of practicing Eastern methods of enlightenment and warrior philosophy gave me inner peace and power. At least, it felt like peace and power at the time. Little did I know that I was in bondage to the deception that martial arts could somehow bring about a true spiritual change in my life. As religious as martial arts can be, this prospect was not going to transpire.

After further endeavors in Japan, I found myself on the brink of joining the Buddhist priesthood, when I began to read a Bible written half in Japanese and half in English. To me, Christianity was merely one of the many religious pathways to get to heaven. Not really an original thought, now that I look back on it. In fact, that New Age ideology is more popular than ever these days.

Several members of my family had accepted Jesus into their hearts, but I didn't feel the need to do it myself. I was doing just fine without it. When I returned to the States, I got into several discussions with members of my family about spirituality. Every time I would make a case, they would open the Bible and read a Scripture which caused me to rethink my viewpoint. "Was the Bible full of half-truths?" I thought. "Was Jesus who He said He was or just a liar?" Was Christianity just a hoax? These questions weighed on my heart. It was the truth that I was after, and I decided that it was going to be "truth" that deserved my allegiance.

Being honest with myself, I knew I had a void in my life. I knew deep in my heart that something was missing. I began to think about the deliberate contradictions of my masters and the shallowness of their claims of peace and inner harmony. I had no subversion of authority and yet the reality of their flawed perspectives seemed to jolt me. I asked myself, "Why are so many of these masters so empirical, so vain, and so rooted in a degenerating tradition?" In addition, question marks hung over the techniques themselves, and I thought, "If martial arts is for self-protection, why are a majority of the techniques and forms handed down so unrealistic and unworkable in a real fight?"

Although I loved martial arts, my perfection of it did little to extinguish my spiritual yearning. One martial arts magazine branded me the "King of Combat," and soon I found myself trying to live up to that image every time I beat an opponent, someone else would take their place. Whenever I mastered a new technique, I would invent a counter. The diversity of my talents as a warrior greatly expanded. Yet I was in a cycle and could not find closure in my journey to find real purpose in my life. There was no doubt that martial arts had a lot of excess baggage, and there didn't seem to be any alternative. On the upside, I believe God was preparing me in some way. I began to redefine martial arts, not by combining ideas, but by creating new ones.

One night, after denouncing the validity of Christ to my sister, she offered to lead me in a simple prayer that would change my life forever. "Why don't you let God prove it to you?" she asked. "What have you got to lose?" I was very skeptical, but thought, "I'll give it a shot." My words were short and sweet. "Jesus," I said, "if You are real, forgive me of all my wrongdoings and come into my life right now." Well, He did...in a big way. Instantly, I felt like I had become a new creature. His Spirit washed over me and changed my heart. I had never felt anything like it before. His free gift of salvation was the truth that completely set me free. I became free indeed. It was like someone had lifted a heavy load off my back and I could stand up straight for the first time. Finally, I realized that a Christian is not someone who claims to be perfect. A Christian knows that he can't be forgiven by being religious, humble, or by trying to be a good person. A Christian is someone who trusts in Jesus alone as forgiver of sins and giver of eternal life. No longer would I place my soul in the hands of intellectualism or warring practices.

From the get-go, some issues within the martial arts seemed unfruitful and I tossed them out right away. Issues such as channeling universal powers using finger weaving, bowing to the spirits of deceased grand masters, and meditative chanting, all had no place in my life anymore. But there were gray areas. What about the practice of fighting itself? What about the use of weapons? Perhaps the practice of any kind of martial arts was an abomination in the eyes of God. Well, that was definitely the view of almost every Christian I came in contact with, and they seemed to have Scriptures to back it up. I decided to give the whole affair up to God and to do my very best to do the right thing. I began to read my Bible and study. Because my only allegiance was in finding out the truth, I had already decided to give up martial arts for Jesus, if need be. I did not, however, want to undo a work that God had ordained in my life, nor discard the talents that He blessed me with.

Early in my Christian walk, I learned to discern between "religious pressure" (to follow what the church deemed acceptable), and what seemed reasonable and Biblical. As realistic as my tactics of personal protection had become, my faith was mirrored with the same pragmatism. Through prayer and persevering study, I came to an understanding that skills of self-defense and life preservation are not only valid, but necessary in our sinful world. There is a biblical difference between being persecuted and simply being victimized.

The dangers of martial arts, I found, are in the abuse of physical skills, the false sense of security people gain after mastering non-effective tactics, their limited view of the scope of personal survival, and most importantly, in the indoctrinations of adverse spiritualistic practices. I eventually came to the conclusion that I would continue to pursue the development of my skills, void from any comparisons from other martial arts. This pursuit led to the formalization of "RBWI" (Robert Bussey's Warrior International). I credit God for giving me the vision to formulate something never before attempted in the long, centuries old, history of martial practices.

To my knowledge, no book has been written about the martial arts from a Christian perspective. The prospect of doing so has been complex, rewarding, and of course controversial. In writing it, I have no avowed intention of changing anyones philosophy. Because issues of personal morality are evident in every responsible individual, I wrote this book to attempt to explore an alternative perspective on martial arts in what is a growing ascendancy in self-protection training.

I, myself, am not a religious man, as such, although I do indeed believe that I have found a personal relationship with my Lord and Savior, Jesus Christ. I want to make it clear that I am not a Biblical scholar, nor am I any kind of theologian. I am simply a believer not unlike millions of others, who desires to be bold enough to find truth in a cruel world. I have found the one true Master. He is not a mystery, or a legend. He is a living God who has liberated me from the bondage of a counterfeit warrior lifestyle. Despite my many faults and flaws, I will continue to best serve Him and to stand tall in my attempts to present the most powerful form of realistic, personal defense the world has ever known.

Robert Bussey

1

THE NATURAL STATE OF MORTALITY

Peace through Enlightenment?
The Three-fold Warrior
The Tri-existence of man
> *The Body*
> *The Soul*
> *The Spirit*
Knowing the Unknown
One in the same?

Peace Through Enlightenment?

Everyone wants to be a wise guy. And people are paying big money to become one. Bogus teachers who claim supernatural powers are everywhere, promising peace and enlightenment. It seems like every time you turn on the TV, there is some new Info-mercial captivating a staged audience with the sale of "power" and even "sorcery." Shelves at the local bookstore are just lined with "how-to" volumes on the stuff. And the Internet? Well it is a New Age superhighway.

A carefully designed advertising program often has the power to confound the innocent and make the con game seem sincere. I'm always amazed at who is considered an "expert in the field" or "one of the country's leading this or that." Most are just authors that assert an opinion and erroneously make theory seem like fact. Among the most dangerous leaders are those who cleverly ensnare even the greatest minds using the zeal, emotional conviction, and a hope for humanity based on deceptive comparisons with a new world order. These convincing spiritualists will even sometimes employ selective Biblical references which help support their rationale. Why are people investing in paranormal activity seminars, astrology, occult magazines, ESP, and yes, even martial arts classes? Partially because of the hope that peace can be found within themselves. But there are many other reasons, as well, which we will discuss later.

People have a narcissistic streak that says, "It's my nature to handle it alone...I really don't need God or anybody." Well there's an old Nebraska saying that states, "If you see a turtle sitting on a fence post, you may not know how he got there, but you can be darn sure he had some help." Many people engaged in martial arts today are confused about the actual nature of their existence and how they can control it. They use a corrupt version of meditation and idol worship as a vehicle toward accomplishing peace through self-enlightenment and a co-existence between body and mind.

Keep in mind that an *idol* is technically a blind devotion toward anything that comes before God. Anything can be an object of worship when you think about it. False religion, the love of money, your work, or even yourself.

Hindus were in an uproar over the mad cow disease sweeping through England at the time of this writing. Their leaders claimed that it was God's curse for eating cows, whom they perceive as a deity. As a meditative ritual, Hindu Tantrism uses sexual intercourse as an idol to lead one to a direct union with the Divine. In the book of Exodus, chapter 20:4-5, the fourth commandment states, "You shall not make yourselves any idols: no images of animals, birds, or fish. You must never bow or worship it in any way; for I, the Lord your God, am very possessive."

In the East, contrasting traditions reinforce a discipline of spiritual enlightenment and harmony integration. What they fail to realize is that these efforts are ultimately fruitless, and in many cases an abomination in the eyes of the living God. These vain attempts, or "works," are but a futile effort to make man a god in and of himself. It just can't be done. It's very clear to the Bible believer that man was not created to be an agent of self-enlightenment. He is not a god and does not contain divine humanity, but was made in the image of God (Genesis, chapter 1). In other words, separation from God is not a matter of metaphysical ignorance or limited consciousness. The problem is sin. It is sin that is the dividing wall between humanity and God.

The standpoint in the Word of God explains that man's natural state is sinful and that all the efforts in the world won't change this state, except a personal one-on-one relationship with Jesus Christ. That is why Christ came to take away sin (Read the third chapter of John). You can't "starve" yourself to a point of knowing God–nor can you "meditate" or "center" yourself to know Him. "Chanting" takes a lot of time and won't help. No physical practice will erase sin. You can't evangelize your way out of sin, and even being "religious" won't cut it. There is no self-effort that will alleviate sin in man's life. It is just there. We were born into it. Again, the Biblical position is that salvation comes to man as a free gift from God. All people can receive it by accepting Jesus into their hearts and lives. That is what is so exciting about the good news of being a Christian. Any other method is considered a vain effort (check out Ephesians 2:8-9).

THE THREEFOLD WARRIOR

The Bible acknowledges humankind as being the highest development of God's creation. Each and every one of us is important to Him. To fully understand the measure of our human existence, we must turn to the Bible for answers. In it we find that God created each man in His image, a tri-part individual. These three levels of entity consist of "body." "soul." and "spirit." This is not an alien concept within the martial arts, but there are distinct Biblical differences in how these entities relate to man's existence.

THE TRI-EXISTENCE OF MAN?

The Body

The Bible explains in Genesis, chapter 2, verse 7 that, "The time came when the Lord God formed a man's body from the dust of the ground and breathed into it the breath of life. And man became a living person." When God breathed into man's nostrils, He put life into the vessel of the body. Man's body is, of course, the outer shell of an individual that makes up the tangible and physical part of his make-up. When the time comes for us to die, it is this shell or housing of our body that is left behind and turns back to dust. Have you ever seen a dead person? Have you ever seen someone killed, or even an animal die? Anyone who has, can tell you that in one moment they see life within the being, and in the next, it is gone. And when it is gone, you know it's gone. It becomes obvious that what is left behind could be likened to a car without an engine...nothing but a shell. Our bodies operate on a "world conscious level" utilizing the senses in every part of our material existence. These senses can be sharpened and developed in a natural way within practical boundaries. The physicality of martial arts is to use the senses to keep us out of trouble, and further, to use the shell of our body as a weapon of defense.

The Scripture tells us that the body is a place where God dwells and should be treated as such. 1 Corinthians 3:16 states, "Don't you realize that you are the house of God, and that the Spirit of God lives among you in his house? If anyone defiles and spoils God's home, God will destroy him. For God's home is holy and clean, and you are that home." Therefore, we should not violate or abuse our bodies. Smoking, over-eating, and drugs are all examples of this. We are to respect God's workmanship in us (Ephesians 2:10) and should strive to bring our bodies into subjection through discipline. The Apostle Paul understood this and said in 1 Corinthians 9:26-27, "I run straight to the goal with purpose in every step. I fight to win. I'm not just shadow boxing or playing around. Like an athlete I punish my body, treating it roughly, training it to do what it should, not what it wants to." Paul was aware that he must master his body. Some martial artists cross a distinct line between "mastering" a discipline of the body and elevating their status to that of "master."

As warriors of this world, we must strive for self discipline and bring our bodies under control. However, we must be careful not to worship the flesh, take too much pride in it, or consider ourselves superior to others because of our physical prowess. For some people their looks, muscles, skills and sexuality are the central focus of their lives. In a way, their bodies have become their idol, or god. This is obviously wrong and always ends up being a problem. We are warned in Romans 8:4 to walk according to the Spirit rather than our flesh. That is not an easy thing to do in a world of slander and violence. Curbing these problems by living a life of spiritual love makes a difference. Our bodies are unique and special gifts from God that should be cared for and developed to maintain good health and a strong defense.

The Soul

I view the soul as the core of the emotional, intellectual, and mental state of an individual. It embodies the character, personality, and willpower of man. The soul is one of the things that make each and every person different from the next. I suppose you could also say that the soul embodies the "self-conscious level" of our existence as well as our selfish state. When I was a small boy, I hated eating vegetables. I was always told to eat them by my mother and for good reason. But I just couldn't seem to acquire a taste for spinach, peas, and the like. So, like many youngsters, I began to devise ways around consuming them. First, I just refused to put them in my mouth, but that ploy didn't work. My next suppertime resolution was to scrape them off my plate behind the couch. This worked for two nights in a row, until my mother moved the furniture to vacuum. Boy, was I in trouble. My final ploy worked, though. I decided to eat a small portion of the vegetables, and then spread the rest around on the plate to give the illusion that I did a pretty good job of consuming most of them. The one thing I didn't consider was that over time, I would acquire a taste for vegetables and actually grow to love them. What does all this have to do with martial arts? It's just a simple illustration of the powers that rule our natural selfish state. Sometimes the self-conscious part of ourselves gets buried so we can fulfill our own agenda even if it is not in our best interest. Obviously, social environment, genetics, and faith experiences all play a part in an individual's condition. It's true that the mind, emotions, and the power of man's will are magnificent creations of God. Without a doubt, we should strive to increase our knowledge through education and study. However, faith in the mortal mind alone and the power thereof, is carnal and neverending.

The Bible tells us that wisdom and education are important, but faith in the mind is foolishness. Paul stated in 1 Corinthians 3:18, "Stop fooling yourselves. If you count yourself above average in intelligence, as judged by this world's standards, you had better put this all aside and be a fool rather than let it hold you back from the true wisdom from above." Because the soul of man has a tendency to seek self gratification, it is imperative that one renew his mind through the Word of God and through a continuous fellowship with the Holy Spirit. Romans 12:2 instructs, "Don't copy the behavior and customs of this world, but be a new and different person with a fresh newness in all you do and think. Then you will learn from your own experience how his ways will really satisfy you."

Many people wrongfully worship their own souls by attempting to manipulate their existence through the power of their mind and emotions, or by faith in their intelligence. This will only lead a person deeper into the deception and confusion that is all too often the end product of a humanistic science. These beliefs, common in martial arts, assert that man is part of a vast timeless consciousness, and that mental skills of focus and bodily exercises will transcend one's nature in order to affect their destiny or the world around them. It all sounds so mystical, doesn't it? Well, it is about as far from the truth as you can get. The soul, much like the body, is a gift of God that should be brought into submission through a deeper part of yourself, your spirit being. The idea of voiding the mind or harmonizing the soul with the universal consciousness is a popular philosophy, but doesn't jive with the sensible view of God's Biblical teachings.

We get the word "psychic" from the Greek word "psuche" meaning "the soul." A non-Christian mystic master will try to find control and enlightenment through their mental and soulish state or through their own nature. But the Bible tells us that God Himself is a spirit-being and must be worshiped in spirit (John 4:24). You get in touch with God through the human spirit, not by delving inside yourself to find some universal inner power. That is another reason that the conversion experience is so powerful for some who accept Jesus into their lives. Because God forgives us of our sins and renews our spirits, He makes us like new people. Real Christianity is not a mental experience, but a spiritual one.

Over the years, I have worked with thousands of highly skilled martial artists. Some of them have been deeply involved in the occult aspects of martial arts in much the same way that I was several years ago. Someone once told me that Jesus was one of the few, so called, "Masters" who could fully tap into the psychic realm. This is silly and unscriptural. Jesus was not a psychic, and did not operate in a soulish, mind control realm. He was God, who operated in the spiritual realm or any realm He chose. That's what separates Him from all of the other major world religious leaders. The significance of the Scripture, regarded as the authoritative word of truth, is that there is only one God and one way to get to Him (through a personal relationship with Jesus Christ). There are no shortcuts, and as many martial artists believe, there aren't several different paths to get to heaven, but only one correct way. In Isaiah, chapter 45, verse 22 it says, "Let all the world look to me for salvation! For I am God; there is no other." In Acts, chapter 4, verse 12 it reads, "There is salvation in no one else! Under all heaven there is no other name for men to call upon to save them." And Jesus Himself said, "I am the Way—yes, and the Truth and the Life. No one can get to the Father except by means of me" (John 14:6).

Another popular philosophy among martial artists is the conceptual or intellectual direction of honing the "will" as a means of mastering one's intentions. To understand what necessitates "intent" in one's movement can bring insight into how one can master himself. It is not uncommon for veteran martial artists to pursue supernatural powers, and attempt to solve the mystery of afterlife through the regimen of martial arts' practices. They cultivate their involvement in such things as "reincarnation," "karma," "zen thinking," "secret teachings," "purification rights," "samurai codes," "ancient scroll studies," "masters," "dragons," "lineage," "duality," etc. Unless one is to completely reject a Biblical comparison, there are numerous unavoidable differences that arise which discredit these things. It is unsuccessful to search for wisdom, answers to life, and God within the natural self. Because even with all the faith one can muster up in mortal man's efforts, when it comes down to the bottom line, the sin symptoms still exist. The flaw is original sin.

Because a warrior can be deceived and manipulated by the destructive and carnal influence of the soulish man upon his state of being, he must be rooted firmly in the Word of God and in his walk with the Lord. He must pray for wisdom and leadership, and must discipline his mind to focus upon a scriptural-based lifestyle to the best of his ability.

The Spirit

The Scriptures tell us that man is not the same as an animal, and was created by God for His pleasure. When God created man, he made him a three-fold individual. Every person has a spirit, possesses a soul, and lives in the shell of a body. Your spirit is the true inner person that came into existence at conception, and will live forever even after the sheath of the body turns to dust. Through it, man is able to have communication with God. It is through our spirit, that we can come to know the Father in a personal way. It is the "God-conscious level" of being human.

When one receives Jesus into his life, his spirit-man is what becomes new, or re-born. His body and mind are often still the same as they were before, but the spirit, or inner-most person, has become new through Christ (2 Corinthians 5:17) and will live forever in Heaven. This is why, for a Christian, it is important to renew the mind through the Word of God.

The non-Christian often judges people based upon the appearance and personality traits of an individual. A warrior of God, on the other hand, will look to a man's heart, and not to what he sees on the outside. This is the same way that God Himself looks at each of us. This is the only way that I am able to love those who persecute me and say spiteful things about me (Matthew 5:44). My old nature wants to offer them a knuckle sandwich, but my renewed mind and God's indwelling Holy Spirit encourages me to, "try to love them and pray for them."

KNOWING THE UNKNOWN

When man contains the Holy Spirit within himself and has a personal relationship with God, it's possible to recognize goodness and evil just by entering into its presence. This is possible because God (as a spirit) is in union with your spirit (1 Corinthians 3:16). It is this fellowship that enables God to link up, so to speak, directly to your spirit about a person's condition or circumstance. God will give his people unbelievable strength and insight to enact His perfect will in a situation if you are truly walking in love.

The Eastern version of "spiritual sensitivity," as it is sometimes called in martial arts' circles, soulishly counterfeits the true power that God instills in the spirit of His people. In my humble opinion, 98 percent of so-called spiritualism and universal energy practices are nothing more than hype and physics. A real warrior is a man who allows God to speak to his heart, in order to attempt to make decisions and responses that are free from illusion, and in balance with the Word of God. Often, true spirituality in Christ expresses itself in ways not fully understood at the time. But as a warrior learns to rely on Jesus, he can become more in tune with the spiritual activities that shape his life and the world around him.

ONE IN THE SAME?

In both "hard" and "soft" styles of the martial arts, as they are called, there are distinct references to the direct use of universal energy as an emphasis to harmonize with movements respective to a particular art. In fact, balancing, redirecting, and channeling universal energy are the cornerstones of many martial arts' practices. For example, Master Gogen Yamaguchi, nicknamed "the Cat," would sit under a waterfall and meditate to stabilize his being with the universe. Are these practices valid? Quite to the contrary. "God" is not, in fact, the same as the "universe." Many martial artists are confused on this point. They think that by becoming one with a tree or mountain, they are becoming one with God Himself.

Some claim that the energy of the universe emanates from all things (plants, animals, rocks, and man). Using their lower abdomen as the central point of focus, these martial artists strive for oneness with the universe. But again, the Biblical truth of the matter is that they are only attempting to get in touch with an extension of God's hand-that is, they are attempting to get in touch with His creation. Spending time in nature is a wonderful thing and offers great opportunity to learn of how God's majesty is revealed in His handiwork. However, the Bible tells us that God is the *Creator* of the universe-the Creator of the stars, the trees, the mountains, and man! (Genesis) If one is truly searching for peace with God, he must turn his back on the deception of worshipping the creation, and start worshipping the Creator.

"If training methods are to be truly pragmatic, mortality must accompany them. First and foremost, we need to avoid conflict with great effort and remain in touch with the kind of conduct that will promote the highest regard for human life."

—Robert Bussey

2

SPIRITUAL WARFARE

Is Warfare Always Physical?
What Kinds of Battles do we Face?
What's the Best Way to Fight Back?
Spiritual Odds
Spiritual Weaponry
The Warrior's Walk
What About Physical Warfare?

Is Warfare Always Physical?

The answer to that question is obviously "no." The term "warrior" is described in the dictionary as: "a man engaged or experienced in warfare." Because this book is addressing Biblical principles as they relate to the martial arts, it is important to note that "warfare" does not always refer to physical combat as we know it. The Bible teaches that people also face emotional and supernatural battles. It further tells us that, by the grace of God, a believer can stand firm and endure these everyday battles, via a relationship with Jesus. Wow, what a relief.

Extremely common in the martial arts, is a symbol of fundamental spiritual change, expressed in two interflowing shapes called the "Yin" and the "Yang." This symbol represents the universal law of balancing opposites. It is but one of many symbols reinforcing spirituality within ancient Eastern military strategies.

On one of my first visits to Japan in the late 1970s, I was amazed at the guardian statues that stood watch at the entrance of the Buddhist temple shrines. They were huge, masculine, demon-faced characters carved in fighting postures, set there to ward off evil spirits and to embody spiritual powers of protection. Usually one of them represented "Yin" and the other, "Yang." In effect, they were in place to do spiritual battle. The ancient Greeks, who were really the precursors of grappling and boxing, viewed combat on both physical and spiritual levels as well. My point is that martial arts has a long history of aligning itself with spiritual matters, as they relate to fighting outside the physical realm.

Christianity does not need these examples to validate a spiritual dimension. There is an enlightening Scripture in Ephesians 6:12 which states that, "For we are not fighting against people made of flesh and blood, but against people without bodies-the evil rulers of the unseen world, those mighty satanic beings and great evil princes of darkness who rule this world; and against huge numbers of wicked spirits in the spirit world." The Bible is very clear that there are such things as devils and supernatural warfare, we just can't see these things with our eyes. How does one fight something like that? Through the power of prayer and the sufficiency of God's grace, that's how. Because these unseen battles cannot be fought with the body, one must war in the spirit realm-arming oneself for warfare spiritually. The Apostle Paul wrote in 2 Corinthians 10:3-5 that, "It is true that I am an ordinary, weak human being, but I don't use human plans and methods to win my battles. I use God's mighty weapons, not those made by men, to knock down the devil's strongholds. These weapons can break down every proud argument against God and every wall that can be built to keep men from finding him. With these weapons I can capture rebels and bring them back to God, and change them into men whose hearts' desire is obedience to Christ." One becomes a fighter of a different kind-ready to face the enemy through the license of victory we receive through our communion with Christ. The Word of God clearly instructs us to have faith and to be spiritually *in shape* in order to effectively conduct ourselves as true soldiers.

WHAT KINDS OF BATTLES DO WE FACE?

In this day and age, we live in a world where life hangs in the balance at every moment. Mankind is engaged in warfare as you read this right now. Some may be physical, some emotional, and some spiritual. How we recognize and handle our adversary can mean the difference between victory and defeat. Man has been given the ability to win battles, if he enacts courage and faith in God. I believe that courage is not always the absence of fear, but it is the conquest of it through endurance in Christ. Paul wrote in his letter (1 Timothy 6:12) to "Fight the good fight of faith." "Agonizomai" is the Greek word used here to translate "Fight." It is where we get the word "agonize" in English. True spiritual warfare is a struggle which has nothing whatsoever to do with mysticism, incantations, exorcisms, or mantras. By resisting the devil and his entrapments, a soldier of Christ can endure hardship knowing that Christ's death was a sacrifice for sin. It is a mistake to think that a Christian can live a life free from hardship. In truth, a battle continues to wage on.

The enemies of God attack every facet of human existence. Although it may seem hard for some to believe, there is a constant war going on between God's angelic forces and those of the demonic. The result or influence of evil power and sin can manifest itself in a variety of forms, namely: pride, disease, spiritism, depression, fear, murder, phobias, suicide, greed, envy, sexual immorality, rage, and so on. The devil uses all kinds of tricks to confuse and draw people into the ways and idolatrous trappings of the world. But remember that man is a unique creature made in the likeness and image of God Himself (Genesis 1:26), and with His help, one can become an ultimate champion, capable of defeating the strongest foe or circumstance-and, in the end, even life and death itself.

WHAT'S THE BEST WAY TO FIGHT BACK?

When a battle is spiritual in nature, that is, a recognized attack or problem outside the influence of our control, then a good strategy is to fight back in the spirit realm by following Christ. Everyone has faced personal battles. Some are relatively easy to deal with and seem to filter away on their own. Others are so monumental that they stifle one's hope and bring life to a standstill. When things seem bleak, it is important to both stand firm and reach out. Not just to close friends and family members, but to God. The standing order for a Christian soldier is the challenge to suffer hardship and endure it with the hope and patience that God is ultimately in control. Isaiah 40:31 gives us this hope when we need relief from burdens. "...They that wait upon the Lord shall renew their strength. They shall mount up with wings like eagles; they shall run and not be weary; they shall walk and not faint." The apostle Paul talked in 2 Corinthians about how he begged God at three different times to relieve him from his sufferings, and he learned to fix his eyes, not on what is seen, but what is unseen, because he knew that what is seen is only temporary. In fact, the Lord told him that "My grace is sufficient for you, for My power is made perfect in weakness." Paul said he would boast about hardships and difficulties knowing that they were temporary, and that human weakness provides the ideal opportunity for the display of divine power. Only through faith that God will handle it, can a person find the deliverance and peace that one is searching for.

In situations of difficulty, man must fight to survive, and in effect, learn to lean on God through faith and prayer in order to overcome any natural or supernatural obstacles that confront him. Philippians 4:13 says, "For I can do everything God asks me to with the help of Christ who gives me the strength and power." It is Jesus that gives us the authority to defeat the devil and to overcome the desires of the flesh. It is not self-control or any kind of mortal power. It is the grace of God. A Christian warrior believes that he must find his strength in the truth and encouragement that is available to him through the death of Jesus on the cross and His resurrection. If you read 1 Peter 5:7, it encourages us to, "Let Him have all your worries and cares, for He is always thinking about you and watching everything that concerns you." What a relief it is to be able to give your cares and worries to God. It's like delegating your deepest personal concerns over to someone else, and that someone else is God. Who can you possibly trust more than the Lord? Does keeping the faith exclude us from danger and hardship? Not necessarily, but it allows us opportunity to discipline ourselves knowing that, "And we know that all that happens to us is working for our good if we love God and are fitting into his plans." (Romans, 8:28)

SPIRITUAL ODDS

Many martial arts have taken careful consideration of the balances of universal energy as opposites. Light and dark, fire and water, love and hate, etc., etc. It is subscribed that this energy is a duality (Yin and Yang is sometimes called Uhm and Yang or In and Yo) that manifests itself in our world. Evil and good interact together, one no more powerful than the other. This philosophy seems to make some sense when we look at what is going on in our decadent society. There seems to be a lot of bad, and a lot of good. But are we living in a world where opposites balance and counterbalance each other equally? Not according to God's Word.

One of my students, a black belt status holder, told me a story of how he had been visiting with a friend (a local police officer) about a special investigative unit within the department which deals specifically with cult-related crimes. Apparently, this special division was formed as a result of a recent increase in Nazi-style Satanic activities within the area. This officer told stories of all kinds of weird happenings within the metro and rural areas-from black masses to grotesque blood sacrifices. After dealing with numerous cases, this officer had become fearful. Not so much of the cults themselves, but of the possibility that evil might actually be stronger than the power of good. This Christian officer needed to be assured that this was not true. Good and bad are not equal forces that pull against each other in a balance. God is good, and He is God. Satan on the other hand, was a fallen angel from heaven, a created being of God. Satan means "adversary," and Jesus called him the "father of lies" and the "prince of this earth."

When Lucifer was cast out of heaven, he took along with him one third of the angels (Revelation, chapter 12). These fallen angels are called "demons." Besides the fact that God is ultimately much greater in power than Satan, there are still two thirds of God's angels in an invisible conflict with demonic hosts. Make no mistake about it, God is firmly in control. All this officer needed to do was reaffirm "who's who," and to trust in the Lord in order to take command over the fear.

SPIRITUAL WEAPONRY

In a world so full of chaos, it's very hard to rely on God, especially when you take into consideration that the flesh is weak. So, God tells believers to equip themselves. Ephesians 6:13-17 explains how to suit up for battle. Paul wrote: "Use every piece of God's armor to resist the enemy whenever he attacks, and when it is all over, you will still be standing up. But to do this, you will need the strong belt of truth and the breastplate of God's approval. Wear shoes that are able to speed you on as you preach the Good News of peace with God. In every battle you will need faith as your shield to stop the fiery arrows aimed at you by Satan. And you will need the helmet of salvation and the sword of the Spirit-which is the Word of God." These are the instruments of warring against unseen aggression. They are not instruments of human confidence, but are divine weapons available to everyone who is obedient to Christ.

Among my most basic rules of self-preservation is that, "being prepared is tantamount in value, as the importance of training for worse case scenarios." Being prepared helps us to recognize trouble so as to evade it, and it is our assurance to be able to endure it.

While teaching in Los Angeles, I received a phone call from a very confident, full contact, Ju-Jitsu man wanting to "check out the Bussey fighting style." I informed him that it is not a fighting style focused on winning a match in a ring, but rather a realistic life-saving method. He was adamant about "taking it to the mat" at my place on Wednesday night. This was not my first challenge, by any means, but nevertheless, I prepared myself for the possibility of an all-out confrontation. Sure enough, in comes this well-conditioned expert with an ulterior motive. I knew his game plan and made every effort to avoid a sparring session with him. We worked out for a while, then, in front of all my students, he urged me to fight him in a combat match. My attempt to decline only fueled the fire of his intent.

Although larger and stronger than me, he did not take into account two factors. First, that I was prepared. I knew his style and his motive. Second, that I was equipped with the tools to take him out of his element of expertise and was prepared to do so with minimal risk to my own safety. This battle of self-sufficiency lasted about five minutes (quite long actually for a no-rules fight). However, I was able to force him to give up and submit over a dozen times without inflicting any permanent injury. At that point, I had his respect and his attention. It afforded me the opportunity to share with him a philosophy higher than that of a typical "gunslinger" which he was living by. I could have lost, but I was prepared mentally and physically for any action that was to take place. I was "combat equipped."

Rebuking the schemes of the devil requires one to leave no stone unturned as one becomes "combat equipped" in a spiritual sense. Living a victorious life calls us to be prepared and to put on the "full armor":

1. THE BELT OF TRUTH
2. THE BREASTPLATE OF GOD'S APPROVAL
3. THE SHOES OF THE GOOD NEWS OF PEACE WITH GOD
4. THE SHIELD OF FAITH
5. THE HELMET OF SALVATION
6. THE SWORD OF THE SPIRIT

The Warrior's Walk

From a Biblical standpoint, trusting in our own resources is but a temptation of Satan to doubt the existence of a loving God. Matthew 21:22 states, "You can get anything-anything you ask for in prayer-if you believe." Jesus said this. As was mentioned earlier, the key to exercising spiritual authority is through faith, prayer, and the assurance of our salvation in Christ. It is faith and prayer that charge a warrior's confidence in matters that are out of his hands. When a non-Christian has done all that can be possibly done in the natural, he has no choice but to stand back and do nothing. However, the Christian warrior has an alternative. He is able to initiate action through prayer in situations that seem bleak and hopeless. Hebrews 11:1 tells us that "What is faith? It is the confident assurance that something we want is going to happen. It is the certainty that what we hope for is waiting for us, even though we cannot see it up ahead." Miracles do happen in people's lives, due to their faith and love for God, when it is in communion with His will. When a warrior takes a stand for the faith by suiting up for battle, nothing is impossible.

WHAT ABOUT PHYSICAL WARFARE?

Since the beginning of time, man has involved himself in physical warfare as a result of his sinful and earthly nature. It all started with the fall of Adam and Eve in Genesis, chapter 3. The murder of Abel by his brother Cain, found in Genesis, chapter 4, further explains the result of the devil's influence upon the nature of man's existence. Physical combat as we know it, should, of course, be considered as an absolute last resort. The ethical and Biblical significance will be discussed later in this book.

Without a doubt, there are times when physical force is necessary in order to take control over the wicked actions of man influenced by his evil nature. In the spiritual realm, we are able to win our battles due to the superior power of Christ over Satan. In the bodily realm, it is equally important to have superior power over the enemy in the event of combat. Where do you think our country's freedom would be today without superior military strength? It has always been, and will continue to be (until Christ returns) a strong right arm that insures the peace, security, and

God-given freedom of innocent men and women. Biblical principals are the foundation of our nation, and it is this basic philosophy that protects us from unjust rule.

In reference to the skill level and ability of a warrior, he should strive to be as physically advanced as possible in order to remain sharp and confident in his abilities to defend himself, his country, or family. Weak and ineffective combat training will only produce a false sense of security which will, in effect, be destroyed in the event of an actual conflict. Therefore, training must be straightforward and disciplined, with emphasis on realism–in order to sustain an effective shield against the possibility of evil opposition.

3

MARTIAL
ARTS

WHAT'S THE PURPOSE?

I would first like to address a primary issue regarding the focus and purpose of martial arts as it relates to the past and present. As you may know, military fighting skills date back to the early cultures of man, springing into existence arts like Greco-Roman wrestling and Chinese Gung Fu. In time, the Orientals cultivated styles of martial arts into an enduring legacy. Japan was no exception.

With a basis in noble supremacy, the aristocratic military characters of Japan, during the various early Empirical Periods, would have never been able to comprehend martial arts as they are practiced today. These forerunners would have never understood utilizing their orchestrated battle skills as a sport or hobby. How ironic that they have endured so long in large part to these endeavors. But make no mistake about it, the *physical* side of martial arts was historically all about "combat."

In early documented chronicles in Japan, the reference to martial arts as "actual combat" is translated by the word, "Bugei," but eventually a change in emphasis occurred. By the eighteenth century, relative peace allowed martial arts to be practiced for its own sake among peoples of lower social status, and the classification of warring technique or "jutsu" became a "way" or "form" known as "Budo." Thus, combat duels to the death were replaced by practice forms that became competitive, with emphasis on customary rank, protective gear, and restrictions.

As a twentieth century martial artist, I have experienced a myriad of sport Budo and so-called warring "jutsu" styles throughout my visits to Japan and other parts of the world. Although many of these "ways" have been passed down generationally throughout history, original warlike skills were severe and indistinguishable in regard to using whatever means necessary. Back then specialties ranged from grappling, combat in armor, spear usage, equestrian archery, and, of course, swordsmanship to which the Japanese are famous. Other special studies included performance with throwing stars, baton, roping, gunnery, chain and sickle. Over time, original warring fight skills evolved into various specialized "ways" or more appropriately, "styles" based upon years of mastery within each esoteric variation.

When you take a close look at any particular style, you will easily conclude which emphasis the art specializes in. Many specialize in foot and hand skills, others grappling and finishing moves. Some specialize in weapons after you've reached a particular level within the discipline. Each maintain that without complete dedication to syllabus, one can never truly master a style. On average, most martial artists believe that it takes between 10 and 25 years to master a martial art. With these numbers in mind, how many "styles" could one conceivably master in a lifetime? Two? Three? Possibly five? What if one were to combine elements of different styles? Would it then take less time? Regardless, the real questions, with respect to any style, remain somewhere in between its relevance to physical pragmatism and the philosophy it represents. Are there religious overtones? No doubt. Does the style (or combination of them) prepare one for the onslaught of an unpredictable attack? I have always asserted a truism that your body will usually react in a manner to which it has been trained. So, what are we to make of the value of classical and eclectic martial arts? Let's analyze this issue more closely and see if we can find a bottom line.

TODAY'S MARTIAL ARTIST

If you don't stand for something, you'll fall for anything. In this century many participants of the arts regard the value of their training based upon distinct beneficial characteristics that are drawn from their involvement. These can include: sports, fitness, hobbies, self-defense, or even a recognition of the deeper meaning of self. Traditionalists commonly link the value of their expression with a long line of history and origin. They find that clinging to ancient forms provides a genuine connection to a noble past. For non-traditionalists it is a struggle to find any interest or sympathy for this viewpoint. Their preference is to strive to master the central heart of physical skill and fighting efficiency which often lacks character-building traits.

What do people really need or want? In over two decades of involvement in martial arts, I have found that, for the most part, people are not particularly interested in performing traditional kata (forms), winning trophies, or wearing belts. Sure, they get caught up in all of that. But there is usually a deeper, underlying reasoning taking place that supersedes the desire to be good. This earnest desire for the martial arts lies somewhere between obtaining pragmatic abilities and accomplishing an increased self image.

No. 1. "The Real Deal"

In their heart-of-hearts, people want to be able to protect themselves and their loved ones. They want safety and true confidence in knowing that if they were to be thrust into a life-threatening situation, they could utilize their skills and win.

No. 2. "Hope And Significance"

Many people who get into martial arts want to escape mediocrity and feel a sense of belonging. They want to feel significant and be recognized for their dedication and achievements. They want to be included. Further, they seek hope and want assurance that they are improving via the training process. Confidence, whether real or jaded, is instilled in people when they trust the character and guidance of the instructor.

No 3. "Meaningful Growth"

Experiencing personal growth is of paramount importance for most of us. For some people getting involved in the martial arts is a way to fill a void in themselves. In essence, they want the benefits of enriching their lives physically, mentally, and spiritually. Later on in this book we will examine these more closely. But initially, let's preface things with some other basic views of RBWI.

TOTAL SELF-PRESERVATION

Because combat readiness is only a fraction of the umbrella of personal protection, it would be limiting to categorize "RBWI" Ardor Members as mere martial artists. Although numerous individuals strive to develop very realistic aspects from this personal defense methodology, the ideal program encases many diverse aspects of self-preservation. A more complete program profiles information and training in other areas such as: Security, Law Enforcement & Military, Health, Fitness, Nutrition, and Primitive Wilderness Challenge skills, to name a few. "RBWI" blankets the total scope of self-preservation in a seemingly limitless endeavor to educate people in proven life-saving methods, and as a result, has set new standards to follow. Their strategies interact with any environment to increase one's chances to outlast a given situation...applying physics, attitude, and faith against the enemy or circumstance.

A MATTER OF STYLE

One of the most commonly asked questions among martial artists is, "What style do you practice?" There is Jujitsu, Karate, Wing Chun, Aikido, Kick Boxing, Arnis, Shootfighting, Ninjutsu, Kempo, Hapkido, and many others. Everyone engaged in their particular art form feels that they have found their nitch. Some believe that their style is the ultimate fighting art. The perception that one system is better than another is highly subjective and should depend upon both individual preference and the unprohibitive scope and effectiveness of the self-preservation methods themselves. The ambition for martial artists to challenge each other in a "test of styles" is an accelerating trend in our opinion forming culture. This brutal prospect merely entertains, yet rarely tells us very much about the effectiveness or diversity of a style for the large segments of the population. The process to find a perfect style continues today, and hence we have what I call "Reality Predators." In a way, these martial artists have stimulated the progression of fighting styles but have done little more than inflate their own claims of prowess. In the end, comparing martial arts styles is mindless debate because fraudulent techniques and ideologies are widespread in almost all of them.

IS MARTIAL ARTS A SPORT?

Tournaments are controlled contests. In medieval Europe for example, warrior tournaments were practiced and were an important part of social life. Today, martial artists want to experience fighting (without loss of life or limb) in much the same way. However, mutual combat and self-preservation are very different. Real confrontations are ruthless. There are no fight doctors or referees to intercede during an exchange. In addition, muggers, rapists, and street fighters never play by the rules.

Some folks get involved with martial arts for purely "sport" reasons, and that's all right if you don't plan or attempt to translate sport skills in a life-threatening encounter. I learned a lot of things during my days as a tournament competitor. The name of my band of tournament buddies, during the '70s, were the "Headhunters." In order to be accepted into it, the student had to survive specific fraternity-type test requirements, and I was the youngest to pass through all of them. We terrorized local karate clubs by appearing at tournaments with our T-shirts (sporting a shrunken head, of course) and our black uniform pants complete with stars and stripes running down the side. Later when I became an instructor and had my own school, I cleaned up that image and began to develop my skills as a mentor.

As more time passed, I became very disillusioned with the concept of tournaments and the detriments associated with them. I would see person [A] beat person [B] in a sparring match knowing that, had it been a real fighting encounter, it would have been the other way around. Like any sport, I learned a great deal about competitive spirit, time limits, instructor favoritism, winning, losing, and things like restricted point zone areas (only being allowed to strike a specific target area with your hand or foot pad). I came to the realization that all of these aspects built "fatal tendencies" in the practitioner. Fatal tendencies are nothing more than unrealistic training habits and the false assumptions that accompany them.

In the real world of combat, it's life and death–not sport. And it was that perspective that led to the development of an "anything can happen" training program. Although contests can promote skill and strategy, a tournament is confined by restrictions. Tournaments (even the ones that claim to use no rules) are missing out on the bigger picture. They don't address simple factors that could conquer even the greatest fighter like: terrain, the element of surprise, multiple opponents or armed assailants. On the whole, tournament martial arts nurture techniques and habits that rarely present themselves on the street and further a false sense of security in one's ability to defend his or her life.

When the challenge to be faced is to be one's personal best, the trophies won are not tangible, but personal. True self-preservation should be all encompassing, geared to demystify the efficiency of a particular discipline simply by demonstrating natural, explosive elements designed to render limited forms ineffective without violence or sport facade. You may be wondering what I did with all my old trophies. I'll have to tell you about their demise in another book, but let's just put it this way...I'd rather have survival tools in my head, than trophies on my mantle.

MASTERING THE MARTIAL ARTS

Does it really take years to master the martial arts? My Ninjutsu Grand Master told me that it would take 40 years to understand his movement. After two, there were no new surprises. Many teachers say it takes forever to truly learn the essence of Budo, in large part, because of the internal factors that they maintain. They see life as a series of occurrences that appear to them in a long "seeking out process" with an ultimate goal of self-realization.

Of course, the Christian view is that God reconciled us through Christ Who died for us, and when anyone becomes a Christian he becomes brand new inside (Romans 5:17-18). But on the physical end of things, as they relate to aspects of hand-to-hand fighting, the truth is that there is no "arrival" to mastering all the variations associated with human nature and response. It is a constant learning process, with an emphasis on supreme adaptability. A trainee should always assume that anyone, regardless of size or skill level, is dangerous.

In order to defend against the brawler or trained technician, you must be exposed to methods that work against armed, unarmed, and even multiple attackers when they are moving against you in their particular mode of assault. You need to develop processes that allow you to assess a given situation, and have the power to act with a conduct that insures your best interest. Surprisingly, these methods can be learned very quickly, if there is no allegiance to outdated patterns, blocks, and strikes, scoring points or upholding memorized step-by-step movements.

My quest has led me to believe that a veteran martial artist can be beaten by a complete novice, and a majority of so-called "modern proven effective" martial arts are nothing more than a scam. We should be ever changing and workable in relation to opponent resistance—no rules protection. We should not be robotic with no apathy toward realism. On the contrary, our methods should conform to any person's natural attributes and enhance that person's potential.

Sharing methods of self-defense to those who lack the know-how is like arming people with internal tools that can't be taken away from them. It's thrilling to see martial artists, who have spent years of their lives conquering their craft, come to grips with a natural and pragmatic alternative.

Recently, I held a private one-on-one combat session for a fifth degree black belt (master level) with over 20 years experience. After the lesson, I noticed that he was sulking. "What's wrong?" I asked. He simply looked up and said, "I feel like I just wasted twenty years of my life." You see, martial arts contain worthless practices in generous proportions. It is like digging an in-ground swimming pool with a spoon. It takes more time than it's worth. You work and work and work at mastering martial arts skills, but as I have said, an assailant with sheer street tenacity can render most martial arts' techniques useless. Practicing limited versions of martial arts with a current of self-edification is the long way to no-wheres-ville. We should use concepts that serve as "equalizers" (such as those used in RBWI)–not for the sake of being different, but are different for the sake of being effective. Are they infallible? Of course not, but they are original, pragmatic, based in Scripture, and so far, way ahead of an increasingly perverse society.

HERITAGE AND IDEAS

Several leaders in the martial arts community, at one time, branded me as a lethal renegade master. I had, in their minds, disrespected the heritage of ancient old traditions by mastering them, and then expanding on their qualities while dispelling inaccuracies. Back then, if you were not following classical martial ways, you had somehow watered down the essence of an art and were consequently labeled an outcast. That kind of Oriental thinking was very popular in this country during the 1960s, persisted during my training in the 1970s, and believe it or not, is prevalent even today. In my experience, superior tactics among existing Oriental hierarchy is devalued and insignificant unless you beat them at their own game, at which time you elevate your status to that of an idol. It's very strange.

MASTERS?

Although I believe that anyone can master a craft, I feel that the title of "Master" is elitist, not to mention dangerously misleading. There is only one Master. The book of Ephesians, chapter 2, explains man's earthly prominence with and without God. Secondly, although I strongly advocate respect principals, I equate practices like calling someone "Master," bowing at the waist when entering a training area, and summoning universal "Chi" power, as throwbacks to Asian social rituals and divination. For an interesting viewpoint on these matters, you may want to read Isaiah, chapter 47, verses 12 -14.

Martial artists who visit me during public appearances will often bow to me. Although they mean it as a display of respect, I nevertheless despise its empirical implication. I always make it a point to denounce this illusion by saying, "You don't have to do any of that business around me...this is America and a hand shake will suffice." From my experience, the whole master/bowing thing is like a bondage. For example, in some martial arts, it is considered a no-no if you don't bow just before entering a training area. No one even has to be there! The perception on issues like bowing and calling someone "Master" are supported by movies like "The Karate Kid," and even by the vast majority of martial arts' instructors throughout the world. I don't make it a point to show my respect to Thomas Edison every time I turn a light on in a room. A lack of bowing does not make one less sincere or genuine. What about as character building traits? They are nothing more than behavioristic impostors...an outward sign of supposed humility. Moreover, they date back to traditional Eastern religion and social oppression.

The Bible tells believers to focus their admonitions *within,* based on true spiritual virtues inherited to them, via a relationship with the Holy Spirit. In 2 Peter, 1: 5-9, it instructs, "...you need more than faith; you must also work hard to be good, and even that is not enough. For then you must learn to know God better and discover what he wants you to do. Next, learn to put aside your own desires so that you will become patient and godly, gladly letting God have his way with you. This will make possible the next step, which is for you to enjoy other people and to like them, and finally you will grow to love them deeply. The more you go on in this way, the more you will grow strong spiritually and become fruitful and useful to our Lord Jesus Christ." I derive great encouragement from a partnership with God's truth. Do you want to be effective and productive?

SPIRITUAL ROOTS AND TRADITIONS

The roots of martial traditions can be easily over emphasized, and I have no intention of delving too deeply into the various disciplines and their inadequacies. I would, however, like to point out a few technical and psychospiritual dimensions associated with martial arts, so as to give you an idea of how sterile many of these systems really are.

To begin, let me point out that most martial arts are linked in close connection with spiritual endeavors, usually Eastern in thought. All martial arts have a religious connection. Many historians believe that the origin of martial arts started in India and then spread to China. The Taoist/Buddhist religions were widespread; and the true essence of physical and philosophical became a divine union of sorts. As the interpretations of martial arts spread throughout the Eastern cultures, so did the originations of the various disciplines, all reflecting the attitudes and techniques of their indigenous peoples.

Years ago when I started this book (I type slowly), Christianity and martial arts seemed an alien concept. Although rarely addressed, it's interesting to note that the influence of Judeo-Christian teaching had to have an effect on martial arts dating back to the T'ang Dynasty in China. In fact, archeologists have discovered copies of Old Testament Scriptures written on silk found in caves. We also know that the apostle Paul and other apostles evangelized along the silk road into China. Although the broadest elaborations of stylized fighting has been achieved in the East, most every culture has endeavored to pursue them. Interestingly, a supreme factor linking virtually all of the unique entities that flourished in places like Korea, Okinawa, Java, Indonesia, and the like, was an emphasized spiritual dimension as the heart of each indigenous martial art.

Around the turn of the century, martial arts ideas began to filter into places like America, England, France, and other European countries. Since World War II, Japanese arts influenced the West along with others. Soldiers began training at military bases overseas, and Asian instructors emerged here in America's land of opportunity. Through printed media, movies and television, a profusion of styles have made their way into our modern world, including many combined systems with eclectic influences. The American martial arts market today is diverse, widespread, and big business.

THE AMERICAN DREAM

Today there are several magazine journals that address martial arts business information. They contain advertisements selling everything from liability insurance to financial contract companies designed to solicit and collect monthly payments from students. In addition to the ads, are feature stories which include successful owners committed to their craft. In a most recent issue, the caption below the cover story read, "Mr. _____, shown here with his staff, attributes his school's success of over 400 students, to a clear understanding that they are not in the Self-defense business, but in the field of Personal Empowerment."

Just because one enrolls in a martial art or self-defense program does not necessarily mean that he or she will be subjected to occult practices...especially in the USA where many successful schools are run more like health clubs. However, there are very popular "success" theories and "mind over matter" teachings circulating about. The agenda is to make the business of martial arts as profitable as possible and to invoke a "feel good" philosophy in the student. Usually, these training schools are very upbeat and formalized with step-by-step memorized patterns and organized criteria. They are often very commercial and work with community leaders toward the betterment of a safe society. The students involvement is constantly reinforced with optimistic buzz words and phrases like, "Victory! I'm a winner!"; and students are generally governed by rules of moral conduct.

"What's so wrong with that?" you might ask. Good question. I don't doubt that everyone needs to gain some confidence and belief in oneself. However, two deceptions exist.

First, the physical trappings of classical martial arts is almost always so far removed from the reality of what can really happen in a no-holds-barred environment of combat. As a result, thousands of "black belts" and "champions" are walking the streets with an inflated sense of what their abilities can do for them if, heaven forbid, they have to defend their life.

Second, the accent of "personal power confession." although valuable in moderation, is nothing more than man's human reasoning to save himself through his own efforts and merit. It is the "I can" buzz words that sometimes go beyond positive thinking. Man has a fallen nature according to the Bible, and adding self-power merely adds to that fallen nature. Further, it detracts from the fact that God has done for man that which man cannot do for himself. Reading Ephesians, chapter 2, verses 8-9 pretty much sums it all up. It says, "Because of his kindness you have been saved through trusting Christ. And even trusting is not of yourselves; it too is a gift from God. Salvation is not a reward for the good we have done, so none of us can take any credit for it." Truly, confidence as it relates to surviving an encounter, comes through the practice of realistic scenario training and positive mental preparation. In addition, these works are incomparable to the assurance of eternal life given to us as a free gift without having to earn salvation. That's how one can cover all the bases, and that is where the true insurance lies. The physical and mental mumbo jumbo offers safety inside a bubble and seems just fine as long as no one comes along and bursts it.

DEMYSTIFYING THE MARTIAL ARTS

What are we to make of martial arts? Violence has reached epic proportions in our country. Something has to be done. There are millions of people engaging in the practice of self-defense and fighting more than ever before. And why not? It's cool. It seems curative and not without merit. It teaches self-discipline and brings a student into a state of humility and spiritual sensitivity, right? Well, not quite. I certainly recognize the basic attainable attributes of any physical endeavor, like sports or martial arts, where an individual can conceivably gain balance, focus, strength, speed, and strategy. Regretfully, the dynamics generally associated with martial arts are cosmetic, at best, and are not linked with the enticement of power and freedom that people think.

Do the practices of the martial arts masters actually give them the empowerment that goes beyond basic attributes and into mental/spiritual capacities? My answer to this is "Almost never." Much of this power and freedom is nothing more than mental focus and mere physics rooted in myth and legend. Some is a hodgepodge of Asian universal interpretation. All of it, without Christ, is an empty promise of salvation through self...a lie that has been around since the garden of Eden.

In order to demystify martial arts, we need first to admit that ancestral martial arts is rooted in lore and religion. These elements are maintained within the structure of many martial arts to this day and are perceived as customary procedure. These procedures qualify martial arts as a religion in and of itself.

Next, and this is very important, we must recognize that the myths associated with them are perpetuated in an environment sympathetic and compliant with each art form. The grandiose accounts of powers beyond the physical realm are notoriously inaccurate, yet popular. Why? Because these powers seem remarkable, and people are attracted and curious to discover and obtain powers of their own. In every claim of extraordinary martial arts ability that I have personally been a party to, I can assure you that they all have been easily refuted by testing the theories with uncompliant participants. But be assured that in the world of mystical martial arts, scandalous activities such as these rarely get challenged. The attraction of "powers" and, so called, "inner-peace" through martial arts is a sad notion to me, because, although it is self-analyzing, it can never lead to a saving grace of the heart according to the Bible. The idea of power is really a self-centered illusion.

For the Christian, he sees these actions as a stratagem for the devil to mislead a person away from God. For the believer in Christ, Satan is the adversary who deceives people without warning. Just as the element of surprise is used when an abductor lures a child over to his car and then snatches him away, so is the course of the devil when he works to deceive us.

A good friend of mine, Bill Dow, is one of Hollywood's great photographers. His subjects have included the biggest stars in Tinsel Town. Of main interest to him, over the course of many years, has been to photograph animals in the wild. Bill has learned a great deal about the behavior of animals and every time we visit, we discuss God's great complexity within the kingdom of animals. Bill was once attacked by a lion and almost killed. If you have ever studied the activities of lions when they prey on their subjects, you will notice that at first, they will single out their prey (seeking out weaknesses in their victim—perhaps a springbok lagging behind in the herd, or even a human walking with a limp), then with great patience and a low profile, they stalk and close the gap of distance. Finally, and without warning, they jolt in for the kill. And here is the interesting part, the lion tends to roar after the predator has won his prey. Obviously, a roar before the kill would forewarn the advancing attack.

Christians believe that Satan works in a very similar way in the world we live in. In homes and businesses, in schools and even churches, deception can take root among even the most well-meaning, intelligent people. This also happens to some as they get involved with martial arts. When it comes to buying into all the mystical bluff, one needs to stand firm and recognize it as a lure. The book of 1 Peter is a short book, really only a few pages long. But in chapter 5, verses 8- 9, it gives us a great warning. It says, "Be careful-watch out for attacks from Satan, your great enemy. He prowls around like a hungry, roaring lion, looking for some victim to tear apart. Stand firm when he attacks. Trust the Lord; and remember that other Christians all around the world are going through these sufferings too."

Over a decade and a half ago, I sat down in front of a blank pad of paper and began accumulating my thoughts for a generic letter that I could send out as a reply to the onslaught of mail I was receiving from Christians and non-Christians alike asking questions about my personal tactics and views toward the mystical and supernatural aspects of the martial arts. Many who wrote to me were from diverse backgrounds ranging from police officers, factory workers, and ministers, to junior high school kids, martial arts instructors, and doctors. They all seemed to be asking the same question. "I want to develop my skills of personal defense in a real, scientific, and efficient way, but am not interested in participating in anything that could be physically, mentally, or spiritually misleading or destructive. Can you help me?" Well, after a lot of discussion and prayer, I decided to spend the next several years challenging my own personal understanding of these issues as I lectured, demonstrated through seminars, and personally answered questions through letters and long phone conversations.

I am dedicated to demystifying martial arts as we know it. You can't imagine the resistance we originally faced as we battled against the upsurge of these New Age abstruse occultic-style books and articles written by top authors and experts. What a challenge...and what opportunities they presented. Thomas Jefferson once said, "In matters of style, swim with the current; in matters of principle, stand like a rock." Not surprisingly, rational people seem to logically discern and embrace the liberation available to them through "RBWI" after evidence and demonstration has presented itself.

Over the years, I've learned a few things about supposed leaders who attempt to baffle, yet mystify their readers. On a physical level of performance as it relates to self-defense, they teach very well organized criteria which seem very logical-especially to a novice. However, the logic is based upon prearranged scenarios and compliant partner training complete with do's and don'ts. What do I mean by all this? Their skills may work against compliant partners trained to strike and fall a certain way. Their skills may work under limited circumstances or against a totally untrained individual. However, these skills can easily be proven erroneous in the field when no rules are applied and an opponent is committed to winning. But let's not just discuss the physical side of things. For these authors/experts the ploy, whether intentional or unintentional, is to entice one with the promise of discovering some kind of personal secret power or freedom within one's existence. The self-adoring style that they use is sometimes made up of deliberate contradictions, self-empowerment, and an extensive commitment to participation. It's attractive. The idea of learning "secrets" is a big selling point in the martial arts.

Among students of the arts, there is often fascination with the idea of learning from a "master" teacher and a hope that he or she will share their true secrets. Masters and instructors often fuel the fire of illusion with motives to elevate one's status, profit, or to retain students over the long haul. Well, the truth of the matter is that these secrets are nothing more than unshared knowledge and, quite frankly, usually a bunch of mumbo jumbo and hype. How do I know this? Because I used to be an advocate and leader in these esoteric practices long before I became a Christian and bucked the system. It is interesting to note that the concept of secrecy in the martial arts has been handed down by word of mouth or by written code for generations as closely guarded information.

In centuries past, as in the present, the techniques of these systems are regarded as lethal. Refuting aspects of martial arts that have been considered privileged and guarded for hundreds of years is not an easy task. Like any well established school of thought, the leaders and participants are usually programmed with answers to questions and demonstrate their theories. They know that the only way you can refute the nature of their defenses is an out and out fight, which no one wants. Therefore, opinions and traditions have gone largely unchallenged within today's martial arts community.

But times are changing. In feudal Japan, men killed each other in duels to prove the superiority of their particular "way" just as the gunslinger did in America's old west. Tragically, I'm afraid we're moving back in that direction, with street-challenged violence and no-holds-barred contests for money. Soon I'm afraid that they will be throwing people in a lion's den and you'll be able to watch it on pay-per-view.

Martial Arts And The Media

"Image before substance" probably best describes the role of martial arts as it relates to the media. The power of myth and the interest in secret phenomena is exploited again and again in movies and television, not to mention the printed media of novels and magazines. A comparison can be made between participants in martial arts' schools and the audience in a motion picture theater, insofar as both groups of people have paid money to become engrossed in the subject matter and likewise, are exposed to illusion and exaggeration. Rational thought is often temporarily blinded by imagery, and little consideration is given to the validity of what's being propagated. Thus, an impression is formed that the fight technique and New Age spirituality that so often accompanies it, which is dramatized in media, is actually perceived as real. Some examples of untruths in film include:

The "GIVE ME YOUR BEST SHOT" Syndrome
An actor can take several bare knuckle punches to the face with little or no damage to facial features. In real fighting, one or two blows can ugly a face very quickly.

The "LEFT FIELD" Syndrome
People don't freeze-frame between blows. Real fighting is ugly, continuous, and ongoing.

The "WHO, ME AFRAID?" Syndrome
In film, characters fight with little fear for their own safety. In real fighting, threat and adrenaline are much more apparent.

The "STICK 'EM UP" Syndrome
When faced with a knife or gun, the movie star easily disarms his opponent. In reality, an opponent with a weapon is highly advantaged and nothing to take lightly.

The "GRASSHOPPER" Syndrome
In fiction, the Oriental master is virtually invincible and always far superior than a Caucasian westerner. In reality, size and strength is very hard to stop when no rules are involved.

Illusions in the printed media are just as dysfunctional. Several years ago I wrote several technical articles for major martial arts' magazines in which I made mention of Scriptural references in each piece. That didn't go over very well with the editors. Any mention I made of Jesus or Christianity was omitted by the editors and classified as being "religious," and "not martial arts." One day I called them to discuss the issue. I helped them to see that their entire magazines were full of religion whether they realized it or not. At first they disagreed. "Let's take a look at this month's issue," I said. After going from cover to cover, we saw articles and advertisements on Zen, Hinduism, enlightenment, the delayed death touch, Chi channeling and so on. Still, they found any reference to Jesus quite intrusive to the theme of their magazines. The problem was that they still wanted my work. I informed them that the foundation of everything that I had developed was based on Christian values. I told them it wasn't fair that they allow other religious materials to appear and not mine, and that I would refrain from any mention of the Bible if they stopped printing classical Eastern religious views. They didn't go for that and subsequently allowed at least some my viewpoints to be heard.

As one of the first recognizable martial artists to publish continual articles relating martial arts and Christian faith, I've been pleased to see many other Christian martial arts' experts come forward with published works. Christ in the martial arts is no longer a thing of the past. Unfortunately, even Christian martial arts are engaging in disciplines with questionable practices. Of course a believer can discern, reject, and modify certain aspects associated with the arts, but more often than not, non-participation is frowned upon and considered disrespectful and equated with watering down a particular system. This places a believer in a compromising position which produces a black sheep effect. The ideal system represents freedom from dogma and empirical demands set forth by mainstream martial arts.

Bussey's interest in martial arts started at age nine. He began fighting and winning awards by the time this photo was taken at the age of 12.

Over 400 years ago, during a period when Japanese controlled the island of Okinawa, local villagers transformed agricultural tools into weapons of self-defense. The "nunchaku," demonstrated by Bussey during an expo for his local high school at age 15, was one of these weapons.

Many systems of martial arts emphasize the development of internal energy or "Ki," and forge body parts into weapons. Seen here at the age of 16, the author is extending this supposed universal energy through his palm strike to demolish several cement slabs—a technique he later refutes as mere physics.

Bussey's search for an ultimate Master and system of martial arts led him first to Japan, where he became a pioneer of the art of Ninjutsu at the age of only 18. The three fingered posture represents unity of the spirit, soul, and body.

Prayers of respect and devotion are offered to the dead in many Eastern martial arts. Meditation, chanting, and breathing exercises are behavioral works used to pay for sins (bad karma) in the cycle of reincarnation. The author, still in his teen years, is seen here practicing his Ninja skills among graves in Japan.

Jumonji No Kamae, or Crossing Ten Stance, was one of nine Ninja postures manifesting esoteric significance in the art. The motions of many martial arts attempt to resonate with the natural movements of elements such as water and fire.

Known for their high kicking skills, the Korean arts such as Hap Ki Do, Tang Soo Do, and Tae Kwon Do involve strict dedication and the memorization of hundreds of physical patterns. Bussey was the first non-Korean to become an instructor in the system called Yong Bi Kwan (translated: The School Of The Flying Dragon), having studied under its only living Grand Master. One year after Bussey left Korea witnessing for the Gospel, the Grand Master rejected his centuries old beliefs for a new life as a Christian.

At 24, Bussey owned and operated the largest Ninja training facility in the world at his Headquarters in Nebraska. His original ideas and versatility led him to create answers to the limitations and sterile philosophies existing in the martial arts.

After his conversion to Christianity, Bussey started "Robert Bussey's Warrior International,"developing his own strategies and methods, which were much more diverse and effective in comparison with other martial arts.

Bussey disarms the stick from his older brother Michael during an RBWI training camp in Dallas, Texas.

The author executes a painful leg submission lock and hair pull on his opponent during a ground fighting teaching segment.

The direct link between ancient martial arts and its Buddhist heritage can be seen in this photo of a temple guardian at the entrance to a shrine in Japan. These demon-like beings are said to frighten away evil spirits from the temple grounds. Note the masculine lower abdomen, the area and central point of universal energy. In Japanese, this area is called "hara," in Chinese, "tan tien," in Korean, "danjun," and in Arabic, "kath."

A strong military defense helps to insure peace in a democratic society. Top law enforcement and security personnel have enlisted Bussey to teach them no nonsense methods, including tactics with firearms.

American freestyle martial arts, considered sub-standard 20 years ago, are culturally accepted as legitimate systems today. Borrowing from several disciplines, these instructors combine what they feel are the best techniques from each and form a modern eclectic style. Some are highly commercial enterprises that seem to propagate new age thinking. However, techniques and philosophies tend to vary from school to school.

Sometimes it's not possible to avoid physical confrontation. Here, James Rosenbach instructs a technique to subdue and restrain a violent person.

Man should have the highest regard for human life in issues of war. Bussey, shown here attacking a sentry, reserves his teaching of these skills to US armed forces.

Proven skills that work against resistant assailants is a standard of Bussey's teachings. Over the years, the author has developed explosive power and control in his technique. Here, he stops his punch a fraction before it reaches its target.

The author believes that being physically fit is an important part of an individual's overall health and is essential to increasing performance in life-threatening encounters.

"Sakki," or spirit awareness, is the supposed technique of developing and calling into action the complete awareness to feel aggressive intent before actually seeing it. This technique is sometimes viewed as a higher state of consciousness and other times as a spiritual arrival of sorts.

Despite its gracefulness and popularity, it's improbable that one can practice Chinese martial arts without coming in contact with its religious origins. The animal-like movements of Kung Fu require demanding practice to simulate, but in the end have very little to do with real fighting.

The "Horse Stance," as it is sometimes called, is a common pose in martial arts which demonstrates grounding elements similar to a tree and its roots. Some traditionalists believe this stance provides health benefits through the process of drawing power from the earth. Many stances utilized in martial arts such as the horse stance have little or no practical defense benefits.

Females are encouraged to use whatever means necessary to survive life-threatening encounters. Here, a woman is able to break the stronger man's grip by shoving her fingers into the clavicle notch of his throat.

Bussey attempts to address every area of personal protection in his teaching. Here he covers a defense against a knife.

Tracking, navigation, water purification, and wilderness safety are but a few of the primitive survival skills instructed in RBWI by Robert Bussey. The author kneels next to a shelter constructed in the Rocky Mountains during one of his winter seminars.

With child abductions on the rise, Bussey requires all of his instructors world-wide to emphasize pragmatic child safety measures. In this shot, taken during a large public demonstration, Bussey attempts to lure a boy (played by his son Collin) to his car to look at a puppy. The element of surprise and a kick to the groin allow the boy to escape and run away.

4

IS IT BIBLICAL TO ENGAGE IN COMBAT?

Martial Arts as a Religion
Is Pacifism Best?
When Can I Fight?
The Anger Factor
What About Stealth Invisibility?

Martial Arts As A Religion?

Whether or not you realize it, you are being bombarded with "religion." If you think I'm wrong, take a closer look at what your Bible has to say about these matters. Many martial arts' systems are building momentum today based on their participation in curative religious philosophies with a facelift. In other words, their concepts are the very same deceptions that were being passed off thousands of years ago—only today it looks a little different and is perhaps a little more vogue and appealing. Many instructors harshly deny having any kind of religious overtones within their art. But, is this true? And to what extent does their martial arts philosophy constitute religion?

Belief and faith are a practical aspect of human life. People put their trust in things everyday. The real question is: *What* is the object of our belief and faith? You see, it's more a matter of *what* or *who* that object is that deserves our trust.

You cannot open a martial arts magazine without reading about some sort of enlightenment, or how you can master or channel your internal energy. But, it doesn't stop there. There are very few books on the market relating to martial arts that do not address one or more of these issues. The next time you're in your local bookstore, walk over to the martial arts section and take a gander at some of these "works" by the so-called masters. Few cover techniques only, and there are some with titles like, "...Exploring Inner Powers," "...Traditions and Secrets," "...Spiritual Dimensions," and so on. What do you think these people are talking about? Although these publications may or may not seem religious, they are in fact, promoting a cleverly non-structured version of Eastern religion. Many of their fundamentals are so liberated, that many people don't even recognize the shrewdness of their overtones.

Even martial artists with Christian backgrounds have been sucked in. Why? The answer is simple. Many of them simply do not know the Word of God well enough to discern what is biblically sound and what is not. You see, the depth of one's belief and faith is largely determined by one's enthusiasm and knowledge of the object. Therefore, some have become oblivious to their bondage to an occult practice and are entangled in a philosophy that is radically different from that of the Scriptures.

There is so much false teaching out there–it's like a war zone for believers in Christ. A while back, I read a ninja book that actually had a section on how you can channel Satan himself as a way to help you gain total consciousness. This is not the norm in martial arts by any means. But in it, the author came right out in the open and blatantly preached to his readers the importance of realizing the devil in one's life to enable them to embark upon a human path. He goes on to explain that if we listen to Satan instead of rejecting him, we can gain self-awareness. You've got to be kidding me!

There is little doubt that the god of this evil world (Satan) has truly blinded the minds of unbelievers, as Paul stated in 2 Corinthians 4:4. The devil will use every weapon in his arsenal to draw people into his cause. His agenda is usually not that blatant. Unfortunately, martial arts has become a battleground.

Many people have asked me how I can be a Christian and a warrior at the same time. It is a good question–worthy of an honest answer. There was a time in my life when I almost gave up the martial arts because of its conflicting views and philosophies in relation to Christianity. I was receiving pressure, not only from a conviction inside of me, but from other Christians as well. At that point, I decided to give the whole affair up to God, and vowed to search the Bible for the answer to my problem.

Thankfully, God is faithful to reveal His truth to us if we diligently seek. I learned in my soul and in the Word of God about the dangers and traps of certain aspects of the martial arts, while at the same time grasped the value and importance of personal defense.

One of the things that became very clear to me was that martial arts can be, and often is, a religion in and of itself. Many believe that participation in their system will actually lead to some divine consciousness or spiritual peace. When we look at the underlying philosophy behind these ideas and how they compare to the Biblical view of life, we see the promotion of Buddhist, Taoist, New Age, and Hinduistic concepts. Even though martial artists argue having any "religious" overtones in their systems, most of them engage in one esoteric religious activity or another–ranging from Zen meditation, to the promotion of "Monism." If you have never heard of Monism, let me briefly explain it to you. Derived from the Greek word "monos" meaning "one," Monism is the philosophy that "all is one." It subscribes to the idea that "we are all connected to the harmony of the universe."

Before I became a Christian, martial arts was, without a doubt, my god. That may sound strange to you, but besides my own self-worship, martial arts was the No. 1 thing in my life. Technically, anything that comes before God is an idol. My body, thoughts, and spirit were all wrapped up and surrounded by martial arts. I believed that I was one with the universe and it was one with me. I believed I was a part of the scheme of totality and it was a part of me. It wasn't until I accepted the Lord into my life, that I realized that I was not worshipping the one true God–that martial arts had indeed become my religion and the central object of my faith.

Years ago, on one of my trips to Japan, I was visiting with a friend of mine who is a ninth degree black belt in Ninjutsu. He was very interested in what I had to say about the Lord, and he asked me a variety of questions about the life and teachings of Jesus. In our conversation, he admitted to me that Ninjutsu was indeed his religion. When I told him about the reality of Jesus and His love for him, the Holy Spirit began to move on his heart and he broke down in tears. My point is this, when Jesus is not the central focus of your life, something else is. If it is not martial arts, it could be some other form of idolatry, such as: money, work, alcohol, or gambling, just to name a few.

Regardless of any martial art system, a Christian needs to be able to separate the physical self-defense aspect, from the potentially damaging philosophical aspect. That is not hard to do when you recognize it. However, one must be aware that a position of non-participation in the occult aspects of an art, may be considered offensive and dishonorable to the instructor or organization. As a result, many Christian martial artists either quit or give into the mainstream. As warriors, we need to stand for Christian principals and use the martial arts as a vehicle to develop our God-given right to protect life. Above all, recognize that martial arts are not a substitute for salvation through Jesus Christ.

IS PACIFISM BEST?

Many people believe that a Christian should not engage in physical warfare. Combat is a terrible and brutal thing that should be avoided when peace is an option. But the fact is, the Bible does not teach a pacifistic philosophy. From the standpoint of the Scriptures, the aspect of personal self-protection is unobjectionable. The true danger of the martial arts is both its mishandling and its anti-Christian or un-Godly views on humanistic inner peace and mystical standards of living. The doctrines and ethical principals of both the Old and New Testaments do not condemn the practical use of force and do not reveal God or Jesus as being pacifistic.

What about the Scripture in Matthew 5:39? Doesn't Jesus say, "When a person strikes you on the right cheek, turn and offer him the other?" Yes, it does, but not in the context of a life-threatening attack. Jesus specifically referred to the right cheek as being slapped, because a slap on the right cheek by the left hand was a personal insult, much like kicking sand in one's face or spitting on someone.

Although loving one another was Christ's commandment to us, keep in mind that Jesus did not live a pacifistic lifestyle, as many people might normally believe. There is a great distinction to be made in that "meekness" is not the same thing as "weakness." The Bible describes Moses as being "very meek," and yet he was historically recognized as a very powerful leader among men, and was involved in warfare against the enemies of God. I'm sure you've read about the story of how Jesus himself made a whip from some ropes and used it to chase the money-changers out of the temple as described in John 2:12-17. He did this using force. In fact, the Bible says that He turned over the tables and drove them all out like sheep and oxen. With the words, "I am He," Jesus used divine force to down a group of soldiers who moved in to kill Him (John 18:4-6). But one of the most impressive Scriptures is in Luke 22:36-38 where Jesus told His disciples to go out and buy swords for protection.

Because we live in a sinful world (Genesis 3), we are thus subject to the sinful nature of mankind. As long as people murder, rape, steal, and attempt to stifle the freedom of humans on this planet, there will be the need for physical force. Action is often necessary to effectively protect our God-given rights as individuals. A Christian who does not believe in self-protection skills must ask himself whether or not he believes in law enforcement officers, security guards, or even door locks for that matter. Face it, without them, we would be in trouble! It is important to note that when confronted with Jewish or Roman soldiers, Jesus never once told them to stop being soldiers (Luke 6:15; Matthew 8:5-13).

Once again, it is because of man's sinful nature that we must acknowledge and establish basic and advanced techniques of self-defense. Jesus did rebuke Peter for cutting off a soldier's ear by saying, "No more of this," but He knew that He was to fulfill prophesy through His arrest and Judas' betrayal. He asked the guards at that time, "Am I leading a rebellion that you have come with swords and clubs? Every day I was with you in the temple courts, and you did not lay a hand on Me. But this is your hour-when darkness reigns." It was the appointed hour for Jesus' enemies to apprehend Him.

We are to submit to governing authorities when those authorities have been established by God. Rules and rulers exist to protect the general public by maintaining order for the benefit of society. To find the biblical principal of using force for maintaining order, read Romans, chapter 13. In verses 3 through 5 Paul says, "For the policeman does not frighten people who are doing right; but those doing evil will always fear him. So if you don't want to be afraid, keep the laws and you will get along well. The policeman is sent by God to help you. But if you are doing something wrong, of course you should be afraid, for he will have you punished. He is sent by God for that very purpose. Obey the laws, then, for two reasons: first, to keep from being punished, and second, just because you know you should." The sword is an instrument of order only when it is in the hands of a godly servant. But when Paul was unjustly facing Festus on trial in Acts, chapter 25, we see the misuse of power. In verses 10 and 11, Paul said, "I have done nothing wrong to the Jews, (he was Roman) as you yourself know very well. If, however, I am guilty of doing anything deserving death, I do not refuse to die. But if the charges brought against me by these Jews are not true, no one has the right to hand me over to them."

It is also interesting to note that the Bible tells us that when Jesus returns at His Second Coming, He will use force to inflict eternal punishment upon the wicked. When He establishes His reign on earth, there will be no more need for war and killing (Isaiah 2:4). In fact, the Scripture tells us that men won't even study warfare but will all live in peace.

When Can I Fight?

To be a true warrior in every sense of the word, one must understand the principals that God has established for His people. Internal bitterness and revenge is not a godly response to a personal attack. A true warrior must remain unshaken in the face of slander, animosity, persecution, and hatred, leaving vengeance in the hands of God. He must, "offer his right cheek," so to speak. However, a Christian warrior has every right in the world to use just force to protect his country, family, a victim, or himself from harm. There is a time to act. One must never give in to the demands of evil and must stand for godly values and moral responsibilities.

God, as well as government, both have standards of correction and reprimand, even to the point of death. Yes, death. "Well," you might ask, "what about the commandment that states, 'You shall not kill?'" Doesn't that mean that it is a sin to kill someone?" That's a good question. The word "murr" as it is used in Exodus 20, is a Hebrew word that means "murder," not "kill." There is a big difference. Most modern Bible translations now read, "You shall not murder." The act of taking a human life is, as it should be, regarded as an absolute last resort. I realize that this issue is divided in public debate. Regardless of opinion, it is important to acknowledge that it is necessary to restrain certain people in order to prevent the innocent from being violated.

Although some conflicts can indeed be won through evasion, psychology, or the power of prayer, others must be confronted on a physical level. God has given men and governments the right to punish wrongdoers according to His law. Although many people don't realize it, the foundation of law in our country is based upon the ten commandments. Without a doubt, man's questions to life's moral and immoral problems, as well as issues of justice and protection, can all be found within the truth of the Word of God.

The Hebrew word to describe peace is "shalom," which means wholeness, and harmony. Shalom suggests peace between men and nations without the destructiveness of strife. "Shalom" includes everything which makes for a man's highest good. Simply put, peace is not simply the absence of conflict. Should all Christians try to live in harmony? Of course. "If it is at all possible," the Apostle Paul states, "live in peace with everyone" (Romans 12:18). But because of the injustice and tyranny that men inflict upon each other, it's not always possible to be peaceable. If you study Paul's words more closely, you will notice that he said, *"If it is at all possible."* It is not always going to be possible to live in peace with everyone, even though peace and love should be our main priority. Matthew 5:9 says, "Happy are those who strive for peace-they shall be called the sons of God." If you are a peacemaker who resolves conflict, you are godly.

Today's warrior must be spiritually, mentally, and physically prepared for battle at all times. Although the true protection of ourselves and our nation is in the hands of God, there may be times when you must personally engage in combat to ensure the protection of your rights as a human being. The scale of force that one employs in an actual confrontation, will depend upon the severity of the conditions faced in conjunction with the ability and strength of the opponent(s). All in all, it is best to avoid physical conflict and to strive for peace through efforts of wisdom. If this cannot be done, one must have the superior skills and powers to nullify the opponents' actions in an effort to regain peace.

THE ANGER FACTOR

My life's work, thus far, has been to understand the elements associated with fighting. I've been exposed to thousands of stories and scenarios associated with it. Avoiding a fight and actually being in one are two different things. Once you're in the fight, all kinds of strategies and mind games factor in. Choosing not to fight is usually the better choice. You wouldn't believe how many fights happen because one or more parties involved could not control their anger. I've known individuals who have purposed themselves to stay out of a fight no matter what, and yet as soon as they were angered, the match was on. Anger can escalate a situation very quickly, often with negative effects. However, if it is channeled constructively, anger can significantly increase our performance.

The capacity to feel anger is God-created. Anger prepares us to act. Expressing the anger is a choice. Most people assume that anger is a bad thing, and they equate it with hate, aggression, hostility, and bitterness. Therefore, to act with anger is inevitably going to destroy, rather than build. On the contrary, if anger prepares us to act, then we can use it to motivate a constructive response. One night I was out with friends and some drunks tried to start a fight with us. Although they made me angry, I used everything in my power to avoid a standoff and I was eventually successful. Afterward, one of my students said, "Man, I wish you would have cleaned their clocks and taught them a lesson."

"Naw," I said, "No one would win in a situation like that. It's like this for me: If I lost, I'd feel bad. If I won and got hurt, I would feel bad. If I didn't get hurt, but hurt them I would feel bad. So why feel bad?"

The Bible talks quite a bit about the subject. We know that God in the Old Testament and Jesus in the New, both were angered. In Ephesians, chapter 4, verse 26, Paul wrote, "Be angry, but do not sin." It is all right to be angry, but not to respond inappropriately by hurting another or ourselves. We are also instructed not to harbor anger, lest it fester and spoil our lives. Verse 26 goes on to tell us not to let the sun go down while we are still angry. According to verse 27 it adds, "and do not give the devil a foothold." Great advice. Getting anger under control and expressing it without losing your rational powers, may keep you from getting hurt or prevent you from hurting someone else.

WHAT ABOUT STEALTH AND INVISIBILITY?

It would seem that using covert exercises would conflict with biblical teachings. Not so. Throughout the entire Old Testament, we find numerous examples of force being used to attain peace. Under the direction and blessing of God, Moses sent out spies who used stealth and invisibility techniques (Numbers 13). We also know that Joshua of the Old Testament also used spies to infiltrate enemy territory (Joshua 2). In the New Testament, the Apostle Paul employed a sort of covert escape from his enemies in Acts 9:25; and Jesus himself travelled up to Jerusalem in secrecy as found in John, chapter 7, verse 10.

The Gospels contain a variety of tactics involving silent movement and invisibility skills. Quite obviously, they should be developed respectively as an extension of one's established self-protection tactics, and not as a tool for illegal operations or for perverted neighborhood hobbies.

As a means of attaining important information, stealth and invisibility skills were historically, and are today, a significant element of law enforcement and government activities. In the home, proficiency in this area could mean the difference between life and death in the event a thug would illegally enter your house. In the field, they are useful in hunting to attain food for the family meal.

The covert techniques of silent movement and concealment are, in the proper context, biblical. Even God Himself directed and planned an ambush at "Ai" by having Joshua conceal 30,000 of his warriors. These types of skills are not only practical, but necessary in many instances to insure the peace and safety of human life, and as a viable instrument in survival.

5

FITNESS

Training the Ultimate Warrior
Conditioning as a Fourfold Regimen
Putting Yourself to the Test

Training the Ultimate Warrior

When we stand back and take a close look at the human body, we see an intricate machine that only God could have devised. It functions on a level far above what the human mind is able to understand. As science and technology progress, experts press onward in their quest to explore and discover the complexities of God's greatest creation—man. Contrary to modern, popular theories, man is not a sophisticated animal as some might believe. Genesis, chapter 1, verses 20 through 26, informs us that God made living creatures according to their kind. He made creatures of the sea, of the air, and of the land. All of them are called, "wild animals, each according to their kind." It goes on to say, "Then God said, 'Let us make man-someone like ourselves, to be the master of all life upon the earth and in the skies and in the seas." Because God made man in His own image, He is worthy of respect and honor separate from that of animals. Man has been delegated a sovereignty or kingship over the rest of creation. This does not make him God in any way. He is a steward who is to conform to the likeness of Jesus (Romans 8:29). One should care and value the body as a sacred place where God dwells, and should honor God with the body.

To attain any semblance of skill and personal performance with the body, one must train it to be able to adapt and respond to any given situation. Because the body will react in the manner in which it has been trained, it is essential that the warrior strive to develop pragmatic and spontaneous skills of personal protection. An advanced level of skill in any endeavor can only come through hard work and dedication. There is an old saying that reminds me of many martial artists I know. It states that, "Anyone can hit a bulls-eye if he shoots first and draws the circle afterwards." There are no real shortcuts to being advanced.

To become a totally effective warrior, one must be cautious to avoid the traps of certain "regimentations." Many times, traditionalism can be the greatest stumbling block in martial arts oriented training. Although there is value in tradition, I personally feel that all too often it hinders the adaptation and spontaneity of an individual. Today's personal protection activist must have a body and mind that is trained to improvise and take advantage of any and all options available to him.

CONDITIONING AS A FOURFOLD REGIMEN

Fitness, as I see it, is not only physical, but mental and spiritual as well. The warrior must do his best to be totally *fit* and prepared in every area of his existence. In dealing with the fitness of the body, one must strive to create a balance through the conditioning process. For the physical warrior in training, this balance consists of four general regimens: Aerobic-Style Conditioning, Strength Training, Nutrition, and Performance Development.

"Aerobic-Style Conditioning" is any activity that raises your standing heart-rate within 65–85 percent of your working heart rate. This will, in turn, convert your metabolism into an aerobic state which will more effectively utilize the body's fuel sources. Exercises such as sparring, running, swimming, walking, and biking are all very good ways to develop good stamina and a strong heart. If the heart is not exercised beyond regular activity, it atrophies and will not be able to function very well in the event of a stressful situation. Participation in stamina-building activities will actually help you to reserve energy and wind which will be an aid to your performance in the event of combat.

"Strength Conditioning" is basically any activity or exercise that stimulates strength in the muscles. Pull-ups, weight training, stretching, sit-ups, grappling, and working with weapons will all help build power and definition. The generally accepted theory behind this concept is that during strenuous exercise, the muscle fibers actually stretch and tear. As they reform in the following hours, they will bond themselves in greater fashion which will in turn produce increased muscular size and strength. A skilled warrior who has strength is a force to be reckoned with.

Diet is as much a part of the conditioning process as any other aspect of warrior training. It has been said that some of the greatest health problems facing man today are directly related to inadequate "nutrition." There are basically six main categories of food components that our bodies need: (1) "Proteins" - to build with; (2) "Carbohydrates" - for fuel; (3) "Water" - as the basic unit of our make-up (70 percent of the human body is made up of water); (4) "Fats" - for protection and a reserve energy source; (5) "Vitamins and (6) Minerals" - as a safeguard. When one examines nutrition, the two questions most commonly asked are "What are the best foods to eat?" and "How much should I eat?"

Most people don't realize that even if they eat only healthy foods, they can still become overweight. By eating too much fish, for example, you can actually cause yourself to become overweight as easily as eating candy bars. The primary reason for this is because of calories. The calorie is the basic unit of measurement in nutrition and is, in actuality, a measurement of energy. When a person takes in more calories than is needed to fuel their body, this surplus will be stored up in the form of fat. In Leviticus, (the third book of the Old Testament) chapter 3, verse 17, there is a revealing Scripture which says, "This is a permanent law throughout you land, that you shall not eat neither fat nor blood." Saturated fats, cholesterol, sodium, and foods that provide mainly *empty calories* should be avoided. These so-called *junk foods* do not provide a good source of the nutrients needed by the human system. Nutrients are chemical substances obtained from foods during digestion. We gain nutrients from each of the four basic food groups. From the dairy group, we gain calcium, which is important for healthy teeth and bones, essential fats, and a small amount of proteins, the building blocks of our body. The bread and cereal group provides carbohydrates which are the main energy source for our bodies; fiber and the B-vitamins are needed for a variety of functions, one of the most important being a sound nervous system. The protein group, composed of meats, fish, and poultry is, obviously, the main source of our protein intake. And finally, the fruit and vegetable group is the chief supplier of the vitamins and minerals of our diets. Maintaining a sound perspective of the foods that you take into your body is the first step toward achieving good nutritional habits as a warrior.

"Performance Development" is the ability to condition yourself to be able to fulfill or carry out your desired goals as a technician. In other words, to be able to effectively execute your skills and techniques when the pressure is on. In the area of personal defense, for example, you must sharpen and develop realistic combat tactics so that you can "perform" in the event of a life or death encounter. All of your movements, whether you are executing hand-to-hand combat, stick fighting, knife defense, or whatever, should be natural, free-flowing, and instantaneous. I try to stress effective reactionary movement based on tested methods that work.

PUTTING YOURSELF TO THE TEST

Overall fitness can only be achieved in stages. You will have to take one step at a time in order to advance up the conditioning ladder. It just won't happen over night. Any doctor will tell you that quick fix programs for weight loss or muscle gain are dangerous. Sometimes it is easiest to establish short-range goals, based on proven programs, that can be measured and accomplished within the realm of your confidence. Create an overall training package for yourself by first establishing practical goals in your mind. Go ahead and transfer them onto paper and include what you want to see as an end result. Then develop a workout program, designed to achieve those goals within the framework of a day-to-day schedule. Once you have made up your mind to follow the program, jump into it with both feet. Don't give up until you reach your goals. And whatever you do, don't quit if you stumble...perseverance is the key.

After sustaining a knee injury, followed by major knee surgery,

I was told by my doctor that I would not be able to perform martial arts again for at least 12 months. With my annual training camp and other teaching commitments only six months away, I decided to develop a program to get my body into the kind of condition that was needed for that summer's activities.

Before I ever began writing up a program, I thought to myself, "What do I want to be able to do by camp time?" I envisioned myself executing various full speed combat techniques, weapons skills, and strength exercises. Because I did not want to take the chance of reinjuring my knee, I decided that I needed to make my program unique-concentrating mainly on my upper body skills.

After I established these goals in my mind, I decided to put them down on paper. Once I had those standards in front of me in black and white, I began to organize the methods I would use to attain these goals. What resulted was an intense four hour-a-day physical work-out program that I followed to the letter everyday (with the exception of Sunday) for over five months. The program included everything from bag drills, weight training, and pull ups, to weapons, fighting, and eventually light jogging and bicycling.

By camp and filming time, the results were better expected. I had actually achieved more through the program than was originally written down on paper, including the ability to execute various tumbling skills, as well as numerous kicking techniques. Workout programs don't always work out this well, but they serve as an effective guideline toward attaining your performance goals.

Remember that a difficult climb often produces a good view. Don't be afraid to put yourself to the test. However, use wisdom when organizing any fitness routine. Don't take unnecessary risks with your body. It is borrowed property and a gift from God (1 Corinthians 3:16-17). Make sure to consult a fitness expert or physician.

6

SHORT STORIES OF MYSTICAL POWERS

Feeling The Intent Of The Blade
The Pyong Su Hang Strike
Internal "Chi" Power Arts
Air Time
Breaking the Wall
Chinese Animal Fighting
Immovable Stance
The World's Greatest Swordsman
'Ki' Can Shield
Spirit Shouting Powers

Feeling The Intent Of The Blade

I could write a whole book on my firsthand accounts of mystical powers in the martial arts. In demonstration of what one would consider "great or mystical" powers by a master, you must first acknowledge the nature of his position in relation to his independent following. The groundwork of any master to propagate his authority is rooted in the nature of commanded respect upon enrolling as a student of his system.

A misleading master often exaggerates his accomplishments and titles and, in the eyes of his students, he is elevated to a proclaimed position of tremendous authority. Such is the case with the Soke Grand Master of the Togakure Ryu Ninja art and his famous "Godan" test. In order to pass a master level fifth degree black belt in his system, one must kneel in front of him with eyes closed while he stands directly behind the person with a live blade (sometimes using a bamboo sword if he wants to humiliate the inductee), positioned for a downward attack. Now, the test is that you must feel the "intent" of the Grand Master and move out of the way before he slices your skull in half. Sound amazing? Well, if it was for real it would be. Believe it or not, hundreds of individuals have passed this test. The hoax is in the timing of the "controlled" downward strike by the Grand Master. The disappointment of the whole event is that by the time these individuals have trained long and hard to get to this level and paid several thousands of dollars in the process, they aren't about to refute its authenticity. Besides, they've just elevated their own status to a higher plateau within the art-empowering them as a Ninja of great spiritual resource.

Interestingly, before there were Ninja Turtles, Ninja movies, Ninja Halloween costumes, and Ninja motorcycles, in 1979 I was one of the few non-Japanese to be accepted and trained in this art. I was chosen by Masaaki Hatsumi to be the father of American Ninjutsu and lead what he calls the "Bujinkan" in the West. I rejected the idea, and felt that I should instead choose a less conspicuous position, and develop a higher standard of personal skills by instructing and expanding on the techniques with a small group of personal students in Nebraska.

After I became a Christian, I returned to Japan a half dozen times to learn and share with the top Ninja masters. I was very uncomfortable with the physical and emotional deceptive propagation of the Ninja doctrine. For example, besides the finger weaving and chanting, the alters of worship, and the total disregard for reality in defense, it became increasingly harder for me to associate with this "art of illusions." On at least three occasions, I politely turned down promotions that, at that time, would have ranked me as the highest non-Japanese master in the thousand year history of the art of Ninjutsu. But its value to me was not as important as superior skill and a standard of truth and honesty. I felt that it would have been unfair to both parties to accept such a position. Over and over, I read Proverbs, chapter 22:1 stating, "If you must choose, take a good name rather than great riches; for to be held in loving esteem is better than silver and gold." All these years later, I have no regret, because I would simply have helped spread an ancient art filled with illusions and caused others to be prisoners of it.

Although branded a rebel, I have been able to debunk the misleading tricks like the bogus fifth degree test. I once made an open invitation to reverse roles and become the "tester" for anyone in or out of the art of Ninjustu. I would, in effect, conduct the same test using a bamboo sword (I didn't want to use a real blade and hurt anyone). I vowed to give everything I own to any master, including the Grand Master, if they could escape my downward strike. I further promised to hurt no one in the process, but I was very confident that the supernatural sensing power they claimed to have mastered would not manifest itself and, in effect, would disqualify a thousand-year-old tradition. Of course, everyone refused. Behind closed doors, a few folks played around with the test...everyone failed. The lesson is simple. God has given us senses and those senses can indeed be magnified. However, the concept of controlling a sixth sense and being able to command it into action is unreasonable. Proverbs 3:5-6 tells us to trust the Lord completely; don't ever trust yourself. In everything you do, put God first and He will direct you. Let's assume that one percent of the time you feel this intended strike and you move. Is this of your own doing? Or has someone intervened on your behalf? If you step out of the realm of the physical senses and into a sixth realm, a spiritual realm, and Christ is not the center of your heart, whose power are you enacting?

THE PYONG SU HANG STRIKE

As the first non-Korean to become licensed in the Yong Bi Kwon Hap ki do system, I had the privilege of working with the living successor to that art, named Man Dong Park. One of Mr. Park's favorite tortures was to force his students to endure the dreaded, "Pyong Su" hand strike. How it worked was simple. The master would have you attack him or grab him in one manner or another. The technique from his standpoint, was to initiate a defense, and counter with the palm of his hand, (Pyong Su) anywhere on the torso of your body. The attack was a supposed release of his internal "Ki" or "Chi" power, (universal energy) accompanied by a deafening yell. The result (and proof of his energy transfer) was a perfect red hand print on your body. During my 13-hour-a-day training with him, I received several of these. Did they hurt? Sure! I guess you could compare it to a belly flop on the surface of a pool. Was it a demonstration of "Ki" energy release? No, it was a demonstration of one man smacking another and leaving a mark. When I came back to the states, I "Pyong Su'd" all my students for fun. I guess misery loves company.

INTERNAL "CHI" POWER ARTS

There are many martial arts which base their product on both external and internal training. Among them, T'ai Chi Ch'uan, Chinese Kung Fu, Hsing-i and Japanese Aikido, for examples. It is commonly asserted that "Ki" is an internal energy that resides in the abdomen and links one with the universal life force. For the martial artist, this "Ki," or sometimes called "Chi" power is nourished through breathing and exercise. The common sensations associated with "Ki" power are feelings of heat and cold, heaviness and lightness, and energy emissions. An extreme case of "Ki" power involves the famous "death touch" in which a master lightly touches a person, sending a lethal charge of "Ki" energy into him (damaging a targeted organ or energy meridian), thus killing him. These stories are mystical exaggerations and totally unsubstantiated from a scientific point of view. I've seen demonstrations of these, so-called powers, and they are nothing more than trickery and powers of persuasion. They are part of the fantasy world of martial arts that entice and victimize willing participants with "claims" of higher powers.

AIR TIME

Morihei Uyeshiba was born in the late 1800s in Japan, and studied various martial arts before creating Aikido (Ai-harmony, ki-universal energy, do-way). In the early 1980s I visited his house of training in Japan as an observer. Aikido is very popular, I think, because of its beauty in motion and extremely passive approach to non-resistance. In fact, Uyeshiba, himself classified it as "non-resistance." What perplexes me is that it is the very nature of non-resistance itself that renders the techniques of Aikido ineffective as an art of defense. Another reason for its popularity is its ethical tones and religious nature. For master Uyeshiba, Aikido was considered a deeply spiritual activity. He would say things like, "Aikido is true Budo...to be one with the universe; that is, to be united with the center of the universe. He who has gained the secret of Aikido has the universe in him and can say, 'I am the universe." Uyeshiba, like many of the great masters, lays claim to a capacity to throw one or more opponents through the air without ever touching them. To the naked eye and even to some martial arts experts, this activity seems like a phenomenon. It isn't. I have seen this done on several occasions and I can best sum it all up in three words...compliant training partners. Fred Astaire never looked so good.

Breaking the Wall

The late Mas Oyama was so powerful that he could knock off the horn of a bull with one swipe of the edge of his hand. He would punch boards so hard that his fist would go through the wood so deeply that it would actually strike and knock down the men holding the wood.

I've broken every type of object imaginable from concrete blocks to boards, to glass, to street bricks. Everything has a breaking point. When it comes to the rudimentary physics and technique necessary to break, a trained individual can use just the right amount of power, speed, and technique to penetrate the object. Oyama's board break truly demonstrated his power...and lack of control.

Side note: I entered Mas Oyama's facility to become a student during one of my visits to Japan. His school was several stories tall, complete with black belt guards to secure the reputation of Kyokushinkai from outside challenges. When you first enter the building, you are taken aback by the sheer size of the school. Inside the doorway is a giant photo of the master executing a reverse punch. These black belts were intense and well conditioned. After a brief introduction, I was forced to watch a demonstration of two instructors bash their fists and feet against the brick wall to show their strength and devotion. They didn't like me or trust me because of two things...I was a foreigner, and I was a trained martial artist. Soon the kicks became full contact against the wall.

Unexpectedly, I was then asked to kick the wall. I figured, "why not?" I let loose with the hardest 360-degree spinning back kick I could throw. Bam! I wish I could say that my foot went through the wall, but it did not. Instead, the large picture of Mr. Oyama that had been hanging there for years, suddenly collapsed to its side. Everyone stood there amazed, including me. All I could think to say was, "I'm really sorry." They made me wait there for several minutes while they disappeared. Sure enough, Mas Oyama had been told of the story and instantly commanded that I be awarded my black belt under him. Because I felt that this kind of thinking was one of the many distorted reasoning processes that commonly thread the fabric of martial arts, I respectfully turned the belt away, never accepting it.

CHINESE ANIMAL FIGHTING

Some of the systems derived in China when Buddhism was brought from India around the fifth century were developed directly from watching animals. There are monkey systems, white crane, snake, praying mantis, tiger, and so on. The imitations of each animal's ferociousness and agility is the focus of each respective discipline. Fighting like animals looks very poetic, but it's movement is too far removed from the reality of real human combat. The Lord made us separate from all the animals, and it is unnatural to fight in the same way a snake, for example, defends itself. History has shown this to be true as well. A tiger has attributes that a human cannot emulate effectively in real fighting. Besides, I'd rather pick my own animal like a cheetah—they run the fastest.

IMMOVABLE STANCE

In arts like "Shotokan" and "Uechi-ryu," there is a strong emphasis on stance and correct posture. Sometimes this technique is referred to as "Ki Grounding." This notion compares the roots of a tree to man's ability to draw power from the earth to make him immovable. The founder of Shotokan Karate, a man named Gechin Funakoshi, (whose pen name was "Shoto." "kan" - refers to training hall) used to stand on the roof of his house and practice his horse-straddle stance during monsoon season. What does the immovable stance have to do with combat? Not much. Real fighting is alive and ongoing, requiring mobility and versatility. If grounding techniques are effective, why doesn't Japan have a pro football team with an awesome defensive line? All kidding aside, a person can visualize rooting himself to the earth, but it will not make it so. I had this discussion with a traditionalist once, and he disagreed, so I weighed him on a scale while he was relaxed. Then I asked him to root himself. Guess how much he weighed? You guessed it, he weighed exactly the same. Later on in practice, I removed his base with leg take downs over and over to show him the ineffectiveness of this particular ancient tradition. He never took offense to this knowledge, on the contrary, he loved it and became my student.

THE WORLD'S GREATEST SWORDSMAN

Few stories are as interesting as the exploits of a man named Miyamoto Musashi. Miyamoto was a hot-tempered kid who developed a very high level of skill with a sword. I find Musashi interesting in that, although he was a Samurai, his technique was not traditional. Musashi fought numerous fights to the death, and often he would strike down his challenger while he was going through all the flowery ritual of the day. Musashi was direct and powerful, and several books and movies have been made about his life. Before his death he retired to a cave, where he wrote his famous book of strategy called the *Book of Five Rings*. I have read this work several times and find it quite informative, but above all, tragic. Without Christ, he lived his entire life in pursuit of salvation, through the mastery of a warrior life that ultimately ended with a question mark.

'KI' CAN SHIELD

By breathing and channeling 'Ki', some masters have placed sharp blades against their faces and throats without having been cut or receiving even minor scratches. I heard numerous stories about this one and finally witnessed a demonstration of it while I was in the Orient. "How can this be?" you ask. Sheer trickery...like walking on hot coals or getting sawed in half. It's true, the master had his student place a sharp sword against his face with firm and direct pressure and was never cut. The secret is the *firm and direct pressure.* If the student were to move the blade back and forth, or use a slicing motion in any way, the trickster would suddenly be known as Master Scarface. Flesh is flesh, and blades are for cutting. Don't mix the two.

SPIRIT SHOUTING POWERS

Or, "kiai-jutsu" as it is sometimes called, is the art of using tone, vibrational energy, and the spirit energy to stop a man, hurt him, or even kill him with the thunder of his shout. The concept of instilling hesitation or fear in an individual by shouting is valid and possible. The American Indians used war cries, and so did U.S. military soldiers in Vietnam. People grunt when they lift a heavy object, and cry out when they are frightened. Women often scream when giving birth to a child, and I growl when I'm faced with a tenacious opponent. Vocality expresses the emotion and intent of an individual. It is natural. But like all natural things created by God, some people assign them more significance than they deserve in an attempt to make man autonomous and self-ruling. Hence, to be like God...to transcend mortality. If you need a solid dose of humility, you should spend some time reading the book of Job. You'll see that we can never take on the appearance of deity. In Job 40:9 it says, "Are you as strong as God, and can you shout as loudly as he?" The Bible tells us that our tongue can be a two-edged sword and that we must be very careful how we use this instrument. Further, it states in Hebrews 4:12,13 "Whatever God says to us is full of living power: it is sharper than the sharpest dagger, cutting swift and deep into our innermost thoughts and desires with all their parts, exposing us for what we really are. He knows about everyone, everywhere." I once watched an exhibition of a legendary master demonstrate "Kiai-jutsu," or spirit shouting methods. When his student moved in for the attack, the master pointed at him and shouted very loudly. The student actually stopped, and then fell completely down without ever being touched. But, I can assure you that had it been a real opponent, the so-called master would have been the one on his backside.

7

MEDITATION

What Is Meditation?

This book would not be complete without at least touching on the subject of meditation, a practice commonly associated with martial arts. In its simplest form, meditation can be explained as a process of contemplation. It is being able to purpose your thoughts to a particular thing by pondering on it. There has always been a lot of hype and controversy over the subject of meditation, especially within the martial arts' circles.

In my training and throughout my travels, I have been exposed to almost every kind of martial arts mindset. Although some were subtle versions of meditation, stressing only the "development of concentration," others were more openly occult in their intentions-encouraging the student to become "connected with the great beyond" or even "empty in thought and mind."

No matter how harmless or innocent these attempts may seem, they are all dangerously founded upon traditions from the East and are not a remedy for peace and control as prescribed by those who teach it. In fact, most meditative practices within the martial arts, are void of any godly attributes whatsoever, and do more harm to the participant than good.

Probably the most dangerous attraction of non-biblical meditation, is its projected image of having mystical properties, which incidently, is nothing more than the "seduction of obtaining God-like powers." This simple falsehood, first utilized by the serpent to tempt Eve in Genesis 3, led to sin, changing the course of human history forever. He told the woman in verse 5, "God knows very well that the instant you eat it (fruit) you will become like him, for your eyes will be opened-you will be able to distinguish good from evil!" The self-interest of man wanting to redeem himself and have powers beyond his mortal self is a clever trick of Satan. To answer only to the self and not God is very popular today within most meditative practices. These kind of mental focus exercises appeal to those who are superstitious, power oriented, or who have the desire to master the "secrets" of getting in tune with all that exists. Because the Bible teaches that every human being has been given the craving to want to know God, we know that every attempt by man to discover himself or his world around him is directly related to his need to have a personal relationship with God. By accepting Christ, we fulfill our search for a relationship with God and it is through Him, not us, that we discover ourselves and the world around us.

But if the meditational philosophies that mask religions like Zen, Taoism, Buddhism, Confucianism, Hinduism, Budoism (a term I use to describe martial arts as a religion), Transcendentalism, and others are unfruitful in the eyes of God, does this mean that all meditation is bad? Is there a Scriptural form of meditation that God commands us to follow? Well, like every other counterfeit in this world, there is an original. God has not only established an authentic meditation, but He has commanded us to observe and participate in it as well (Joshua 1:6-8).

THE BIBLICAL VIEW OF MEDITATION

First of all, it is important to acknowledge that our lives should be directed by the laws of God, rather than the traditions of men. James, who was a brother of Jesus, gave very practical instructions for the Christian lifestyle. "For if a person just listens and doesn't obey, he is like a man looking at his face in a mirror; as soon as he walks away, he can't see himself anymore or remember what he looks like. But if anyone keeps looking steadily into God's law for free men, he will not only remember it but he will do what it says, and God will greatly bless him in everything he does" (James, chapter 1, verses 23-25).

The Biblical view of meditation advocates the process of filling our thoughts with the ways and things of God, and is not a process of blanking the mind or centering into an altered state of being. One reason I follow the Christian approach to meditation is because it is the only legitimate kind of meditation that God wants us to be involved with. Through it, I am consumed by the illumination of God's ways—how He thinks, operates—and how I can reveal Him in my life.

VARIATIONS OF MEDITATION

Although most people don't realize it, they are involved in various forms of meditation on an everyday basis. Everything a person looks at, thinks about, imagines, mutters, laughs, cries, or speaks, has a direct link with the condition of his or her soul and is a type of meditation. Man's personality and outlook is shaped and molded by the kinds of things he meditates on. It is for this reason that God warns us to be cautious of the dangers of what our senses take in. For example, Jesus spoke of the eyes as being a kind of gateway to the soul in Luke 11:33. He explained that man cannot hide the true state of his heart and personality. The bottom line is this: Whatever we look at, we tend to think about, and the kinds of things that float around in our minds can later manifest themselves in our lifestyles. Our emotions, feelings, and thoughts are all linked with the kinds of things we set our eyes upon-the kinds of things we meditate on. As a Christian, one must try his very best to keep his eyes off of the standards of the world, and keep them on the things of God, lest he become distracted. Throughout the Scriptures, we are constantly instructed to guard our senses and to be careful of the things we focus on.

HOW CAN I ATTAIN WISDOM?

The biblical concept of meditation unmasks a version designed, not just to increase our knowledge, but to reveal to us God's Word in its deepest form. One of the greatest results of Christian-oriented meditation, is the reward of wisdom. Ecclesiastes 10:2 states that, "A wise man's heart leads him to do right, and a fool's heart leads him to do evil." And in Proverbs 21:22 we learn that, "A wise man conquers the strong man and levels his defenses." In fact, there are literally dozens and dozens of Scriptures relating to the attainment of wisdom, all of which stem from a basic level of humility before God. Solomon, who was said to be the wisest man who ever lived, put it this way, "How does a man become wise? The first step is to trust and reverence the Lord!"

As believers, we must keep in mind that wisdom is not the same thing as knowledge. Wisdom is basically from the heart and knowledge is from the mind. Wisdom comes to us through the initial conception of thought, which is the step that comes before the meditational process. In other words, something has to start in your mind, and then be transferred to your heart by meditating on it. Once this process takes place, the end result will be wisdom. I once heard a minister say that, "Knowledge without God only produces intellectual barbarians." The Scriptural approach to meditation is to bring alive the truth of God's Word in every facet of your being. Meditation without the Lord can actually separate a well-meaning individual from God. Believers in a risen Savior are not commanded to sit down, hum, shave their heads, or tie their legs up like pretzels. They are, however, instructed to contemplate on those things which are right in the sight of God and bring them into a place of rest within their hearts. This "pruning" process will bring about the kind of wisdom needed to sustain good judgment in all matters of life.

8

FINAL THOUGHTS

CONCLUSION

Martial arts is warfare. A strategy of man vs. man. Defense is a countermeasure to aggression and an act of protection from danger. What can be said about the way people treat each other? No one can dispute man's long and ancient history of carrying out appalling acts against fellow human beings. Sadly, there is not a single place on this earth where people can live out their lives totally liberated from the ill-effects of man's nature to commit sin. Not one single place. However, as bleak as this sin factor seems to be, we have been given an inheritance to bridge the gap between us and a changeless, perfect God. "You were lost, without God, without hope. But now you belong to Christ Jesus, and though you once were far away from God, now you have been brought very near to him because of what Jesus Christ has done for you with his blood. For Christ himself is our way of peace." Ephesians 2:12-14. Our release from sin is a gift and our union with Christ reshapes our perspective of this world.

It is obvious, and I have tried to show throughout this book that no man can save his own soul. Not through paganism, self-awareness, or holistic health. Further, no man has powers beyond those of a mortal state of being. No matter how hard we try to raise our status beyond that of a human, or utilize forces outside of God's plan for man to cultivate his abilities, the fact remains that people will never be anything more or less than imperfect persons.

One must recognize that any effort on our part to erase the inherent defect of sin within our nature through self-sacrifice or practice, is futile. It cannot be done. The upside is that our being saved is a free gift available to us from a loving, personal God. Simply put, it is belief in the death and resurrection of Jesus that is God's plan to forgive sinful people. Romans 10:9 tells us, "For if you tell others with your own mouth that Jesus Christ is your Lord, and believe in your own heart that God has raised him from the dead, you will be saved."

What elevates Christianity above all other world religions is the undeniable historical fact that Jesus was raised from the dead. Not so for Buddha, Confucius, or Mohammed. In the 15th Chapter of 1 Corinthians, Paul explained that if Christ had not been raised from the dead, than our faith is futile and we are still in sin. Mankind's freedom from sin is directly linked to the empty tomb of Jesus, and cannot be found in anyone or anything else. The Bible tells us in Acts 4:12 that, "There is salvation in no one else! Under all heaven there is no other name for men to call upon to save them." That is a bold statement.

Does our salvation then shield us from conflict in a misguided world? Not completely. Persecution, cruelty, and evil are facts of life. Ever since God created man, He has given him the freedom to choose between good and evil. God intends for us to resist evil and overcome it through our relationship with Jesus. In addition, it is important to be prepared to resolve conflicts with action. In the Old Testament, Joshua did not have to fight when he went to Jericho, but he was prepared for battle nonetheless.

Should our children, wives, and loved ones be armed with the knowledge and skills associated with self-preservation? Absolutely. Danger to humanity takes on many forms. To be skeptical of realistic life-saving practices would negate biblical standards, as well as common sense. Any decision to engage in combat must be based upon the need to survive rather than revenge, panic, or ego. Often it is not external circumstances which cause fighting, but rather internal conflicts and motives which lead to trouble. In these cases it takes humility, confidence, and the desire to be a peacemaker, in order to divert the escalation of petty conflicts. Matthew 5:9 reminds us, "Happy are those who strive for peace-they shall be called sons of God." To be a person God can bless, we must make every effort to live at peace with everyone and to do what leads to peace as instructed in Romans 12:18 and 14:19.

A final word of caution to Christians and non-Christians alike. Your participation in martial arts for reasons other than sheer personal defense may require reflection. Martial arts often align themselves with matters relating to the spirit. Good intentions could be an invitation to deception on your physical, mental, and spiritual well-being. In John 14:27, Christ's parting message was, "I am leaving you with a gift-peace of mind and heart! And the peace I give isn't fragile like the peace the world gives. So don't be troubled or afraid." Currently, there are literally thousands of distinct Christian denominations in the world. However, becoming a Christian is easy. God loves you and wants a personal relationship with you. The challenge is yours.